AUTHOR

HANNON, P.

CLASS

COSI

TITLE   The Furness Way

D0230680

HILLSIDE GUIDES

■ *Walking Country*
ILKLEY MOOR   **NIDDERDALE**
BOWLAND   **TEESDALE**
      MALHAMDALE

■ *Pub Walks* by Valerie Yewdall
HARROGATE/WHARFE VALLEY
HAWORTH/AIRE VALLEY

■ *Long Distance Walks*
THE FURNESS WAY
THE COAST TO COAST WALK
DALES WAY COMPANION
CLEVELAND WAY COMPANION
THE WESTMORLAND WAY
THE CUMBERLAND WAY
NORTH BOWLAND TRAVERSE (David Johnson)

■ *Large format colour hardback*
FREEDOM OF THE DALES

■ *Circular Walks - Yorkshire Dales*
WALKS IN WHARFEDALE
WALKS IN THREE PEAKS COUNTRY
WALKS IN WENSLEYDALE
WALKS IN SWALEDALE
WALKS ON THE HOWGILL FELLS

■ *Circular Walks - North York Moors*
BOOK ONE - WESTERN MOORS
BOOK TWO - SOUTHERN MOORS
BOOK THREE - NORTHERN MOORS

■ *Circular Walks - South Pennines*
WALKS IN BRONTE COUNTRY
WALKS IN CALDERDALE

■ *Hillwalking - Lake District*
OVER LAKELAND MOUNTAINS
OVER LAKELAND FELLS

■ *Biking Country*
YORKSHIRE DALES CYCLE WAY (Richard Peace)

80 DALES WALKS - an omnibus *(Cordee, Leicester)*

■**WALKING COUNTRY TRIVIA QUIZ**■
1000 questions on the great outdoors

WALKING COUNTRY

FURNESS WAY

Paul Hannon

HILLSIDE

0634931 1

HILLSIDE
PUBLICATIONS
11 Nessfield Grove
Keighley
West Yorkshire
BD22 6NU

First published 1984
Revised Edition 1994

© Paul Hannon 1984, 1994

ISBN 1 870141 27 X

Whilst the author has walked and researched the entire route for the purposes of this guide, no responsibility can be accepted for any unforeseen circumstances encountered while following the walk. The publisher would, however, greatly appreciate any information regarding material changes to the route, and any problems encountered.

Cover Photographs:
Paul Hannon/Big Country Picture Library
(see page 104)

Page One illustration: Grassguards Gill

The maps in this book are based upon the
1900-1930 Ordnance Survey 1:10,560 (6-inch) maps

Printed in Great Britain by
Carnmor Print and Design
95-97 London Road
Preston
Lancashire
PR1 4BA

CONTENTS

On Lord's Seat, Whitbarrow

INTRODUCTION

This book is a guide to a 75 mile long walk across southern Lakeland, from Arnside on the eastern side of Morecambe Bay, to Ravenglass on the Irish Sea. The aim of the route is to cross the southern Lake District (most of which is free from mass tourism) by traversing a good deal of the old county of Lancashire, North of the Sands. The main portion of this once detached part of Lancashire has been known for centuries as Furness, and no doubt will continue to be, particularly the lower country south of the Lake District proper. To complete the old county is the Cartmel peninsula to the east, a Furness in miniature.

Despite its allegiance to Furness, the walk actually begins in old Westmorland and finishes in old Cumberland - both snatch a day at each end of the walk. The Furness Way does, of course, link up with two other Cumbrian routes, namely the Westmorland Way, which runs for 98 miles from Appleby to Arnside, and the Cumberland Way, which completes the triangle by way of an 80 mile route from Ravenglass to Appleby.

As long distance trails go, the Furness Way is by and large a generally easy walk (certainly in northern terms, at least), and perhaps the best idea is to use the six daily sections as set out in the following pages. This ensures a modest average of 12½ miles per day. This is unlikely to be too short for most walkers carrying decent sized packs, as there are many little ups and downs (and one or two bigger ones) and much of interest to delay the observant walker. The terrain is in fact incredibly varied, from wide estuaries to mountain passes, and incorporating most other things in between these two extremities.

The Way begins in the Silverdale/Arnside Area of Outstanding Natural Beauty, passing through limestone country of the highest order. The rich woodland proves to be a dominant feature of the walk ahead. Famous old houses and rolling parkland lead into an unfrequented corner of the Lake District

National Park. The Lyth Valley is followed by the shy Winster Valley, with the outstanding limestone fells of Whitbarrow and Hampsfell being traversed. Cartmel, where its cluster of houses shelter beneath the great priory, is a wonderful place to break journey. Beyond, an undulating ridge leads to the outflow from Windermere, and a return to the estuaries of Morecambe Bay. The Crake Valley and its unassuming villages start a bee-line for Coniston Water, but the lonely heights of Bethecar Moor await, with bird's-eye views over the lake. Finally bustling Coniston is reached, beneath the real mountains. An ancient packhorse route leads effortlessly to the 2000ft contour to give access to the delights of the Duddon Valley, and a lower fell crossing gains the threshold of the final stage, incomparable Eskdale. The joys of the river Esk precede the final leg, one last mini-mountain as Muncaster Fell ensures a worthy finale before descent to Muncaster Castle and the coast.

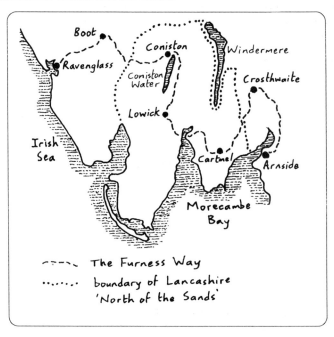

PLANNING THE WALK

Each suggested overnight halt is at a location providing several kinds of accommodation. The two largest communities, Arnside and Coniston, have ample places, and both also have youth hostels. Cartmel and Ravenglass have a handful of B + B's and larger hotels, while Crosthwaite and Boot each have a number of B + B's, the latter also having a youth hostel nearby. Lowick is rather limited. If struggling, the alternatives are either to catch the infrequent Coniston bus for a bed elsewhere, or break journey earlier, perhaps at Greenodd.

A simple accommodation list is freely available to purchasers of the guide, *please send a SAE to the publisher*. It is not intended to be comprehensive, but does include numerous addresses in locations which may be hard to find elsewhere.

Access to the terminal points is easiest by rail. Both Arnside and Ravenglass have their own stations - the only two on the route, in fact. Both are connected to Carnforth on the West Coast main line, while Ravenglass is linked directly to Carlisle, to the north.

If this six-day itinerary leaves one with a day to spare, consider spending it in Eskdale. Here one could abandon the big pack for the day, and if suitable, venture into the crucible of England's hills, the upper reaches of the Esk. The suitably equipped and experienced might then venture onto the high tops, perhaps Bowfell, Scafell or Scafell Pike itself, the roof of England. On the other hand, a day on the steam railway combined with gentle strolls and the welcoming pubs of Eskdale also has its merits!

ORDNANCE SURVEY MAPS

Highly recommended are the following two Landranger sheets
        96 - *South Lakeland*   97 - *Kendal to Morecambe*
Sheet 89, *West Cumbria* also includes a small section of Eskdale. These excellent maps cover the entire route, and make ideal companions to the guide. They give an incomparable overview of southern Lakeland, and are essential in identifying short-cuts, detours, optional extras and public transport links.

SOME USEFUL FACILITIES

This is a general guide only

	Youth Hostel	other accom.	pub or hotel	bus route	Post office	other shop	public toilets	phone box
Arnside	*	*	*	*	*	*	*	*
Milnthorpe		*	*	*	*	*	*	*
Heversham		*	*	*	*			*
Levens Bridge				*				
Sizergh			*					
Brigsteer		*	*					*
Underbarrow		*	*					*
Crosthwaite		*	*		*			*
Witherslack		*						
Lindale		*	*	*	*		*	*
Cartmel		*	*	*	*	*	*	*
Haverthwaite		*	*	*				*
Greenodd		*	*	*	*	*	*	*
Penny Bridge			*	*				*
Spark Bridge		*	*	*				*
Lowick Green			*	*				*
Lowick Bridge		*	*	*				*
Coniston Water		*		*			*	
Coniston	*	*	*	*	*	*	*	*
Seathwaite		*	*	*				*
Boot	*	*	*		*	*	*	*
Eskdale Green		*	*	*	*	*	*	*
Ravenglass		*	*	*	*	*	*	*

THE COUNTRY CODE

Respect the life and work of the countryside
Protect wildlife, plants and trees
Keep to public paths across farmland
Safeguard water supplies
Go carefully on country roads
Keep dogs under control
Guard against all risks of fire
Fasten all gates
Leave no litter - take it with you
Make no unnecessary noise
Leave livestock, crops and machinery alone
Use gates, stiles to cross fences, hedges, walls

SOME USEFUL ADDRESSES

Ramblers' Association
1/5 Wandsworth Road, London SW8 2XX
Tel. 0171-582 6878

Tourist Information

29 Castle Hill, **Lancaster** LA1 1YN   Tel. 01524-32878

Victoria Hall, Main Street, **Grange over Sands** LA11 6PT
Tel. 015395-34026

Coronation Hall, County Square, **Ulverston** LA12 7LZ
Tel. 01229-57120

16 Yewdale Road, **Coniston** LA21 8DU   Tel. 015394-41533

Ravenglass & Eskdale Railway, **Ravenglass** CA18 1SW
Tel. 01229-717278

Lake District National Park Visitors Services
Brockhole, Windermere LA23 2AQ
Tel. 015394-46601

Youth Hostels Association
Trevelyan House, St. Albans, Herts. AL1 2DY
Tel. 01727-55215

Cumbria County Transport Information
Tel. 01228-812812

Cumberland Motor Services   Tel. 01946-63222

British Rail: Carlisle - 01228-44711
Barrow - 01229-821805   **Lancaster** - 01524-32333

Friends of the Lake District
No. 3, Yard 77, Highgate, Kendal LA9 4ED
Tel. 01539-720788 *(not an information service)*

Lake District Weather Forecast   Tel. 017687-75757

The Route Guide

The main body of this guide is a detailed companion to the route, stretching from page 12 to page 99. The maps take the form of one continuous strip-map, flowing from one double page spread to the next. Thus, while the guide is divided into six convenient sections, it is just as easy to plan one's own sections. With a couple of exceptions, the maps are to be found on right-hand pages. On the same or facing page is the running commentary, with a detailed description of the route highlighted in bold. This is supplemented by countless notes, diagrams and illustrations on features of interest along the way.

The maps are on an approximate scale of 2½ inches to the mile, and the top of the page is always north.

Key to the map symbols

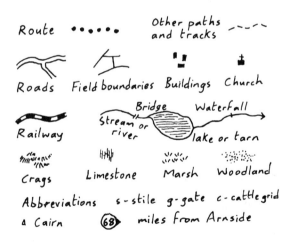

SECTION 1

—— ARNSIDE TO CROSTHWAITE ——

15 miles   1475 feet of ascent

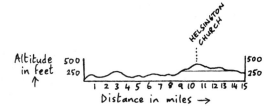

The first day is also the longest, though the distance is hardly overfacing in view of the mild nature of the terrain. It is, in fact, a veritable cultural extravaganza. Passed en route are some splendid old buildings, from the ruinous pele at Hazelslack to the grandeur of Sizergh Castle, Dallam Tower and Levens Hall. The Way also takes in the serene parklands of the latter two, along with fine views from the modest heights of Holeslack and Helsington church. Limestone plays a major part in this landscape.

Anglian cross,
Heversham

Always a bright and breezy settlement, Arnside stands on the shoreline of Morecambe Bay, where the waters of the river Kent merge into it. There are no gaudy seaside entertainments here, just attractions that are strictly natural. The exception to this is the mighty Kent Viaduct, which carries the railway to Furness over 50 arches high above the estuary. A train pulling out of the station always attracts the interest of visitors, who will watch it chug over every arch. Most of interest in the village itself is spread along the front, in the shape of two hotels and an assortment of shops and cafes, though there are more of these further up the road, where our walk turns into the hinterland of the village.

Above the houses Arnside Knott rises over 500 feet, and as would be expected, is an excellent viewpoint. It is also the summit of the Silverdale/Arnside Area of Outstanding Natural Beauty, which has its base in the village. This entirely gorgeous tract of land is typified by the rich tangle of limestone outcrops and walls, lush pastures, mixed woodland and fascinating seashore.

The pier was constructed by the Ulverston & Lancaster Railway Company to provide a wharf for sea-borne traffic, as construction of their viaduct now prevented ships from reaching the port of Milnthorpe. The end section was destroyed by storm in 1934, and rebuilt by the railway's then owners, the London, Midland & Scottish. Subsequently it was bought by the parish council, but was again ripped apart by storms in the winter of 1982/83. It was restored to first class condition by virtue of £25,000 raised largely by the efforts of the local community, and was re-opened on 12th April 1984. Take a long look across the bay: far into the hazy distance, beyond countless intervening hills and valleys, is journey's end.

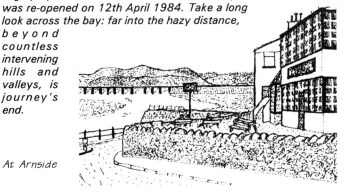

At Arnside

The Furness Way commences on the front at Arnside. An ideal starting point is the pier, which although tiny may be recognised instantly by its surrounding of weary Westmorland Wayfarers sighing with relief and muttering "never again". They don't really mean that of course, for who knows, maybe one of them is going to keep himself active by setting out on the wonderful Furness Way tomorrow?

From the pier turn right along the front, (i.e. with the water on your right) and when the main road (Silverdale Road) climbs away from the front, follow it up through the village. After levelling out the road swings right by the Catholic church of Our Lady of Lourdes: here leave it by going straight ahead along Briery Bank.

A lovely orchard is passed, and views are enjoyed over Hutton Roof Crags to the first sighting - this one a mere glimpse - of the flat top of Ingleborough. The easternmost fells of Lakeland also make their appearance over the estuary. **The road descends to a T-junction with Black Dyke Road.**

Cross straight over and escape down a short-lived lane opposite, to reach the railway line flanked by wicket-gates. An enclosed path heads straight across the field, leading to a crossing of a murky drain. It continues across Arnside Moss to a similar situation at the end of the next field, where at 6am one spring morning a large fox strode as bold as brass alongside me. **A very large field is then crossed to a hedge at the far end.** Note the embowered way going off to the left, and look back through the gap to see the houses of Arnside sheltering beneath the wooded Knott. **A smaller field leads to a stile into a narrow lane.**

The gap-stile straight across could cause agony to any chunky fellow walkers: from it cross the field to some small limestone outcrops towards a gate at the far end. Then, however, ignore the gate in favour of a gap-stile in the wall on the right. Turn left a few yards to another gap-stile by a gate. Pass through it and go forward to join a farm track which is followed to the far end of the field (often used by caravanners). **Just ahead stands Hazelslack pele tower, which is reached by turning right along the lane.**

Enter the farmyard at Hazelslack, and after gazing at the old tower, take a stile to the right of the house to enter a field. Head for the far side to locate a well hidden stile 25 yards to the right of a telegraph pole. It admits to another narrow lane.

On the approach to Hazelslack the route coincides with that of the
Westmorland Way. This acquaintance lasts only a few minutes.

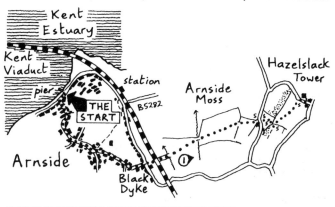

Hazelslack Tower stands in the corner of a farmyard, but despite
its ruinous state and acquisition of foliage, still looks impressive.
Like many others in the vicinity, it was built in the late 14th
century to afford protection from the marauding Scots who were
always likely to drop by.

Hazelslack Tower

15

Leave the lane by a stile straight ahead, and follow a track away. When it swings right to become enclosed by walls, bear left to an interesting stile, fronted with stone steps, in the wall corner. Navigation now eases for a good while: from the stile simply follow the wall on the left. Here we are almost entirely enclosed by natural woodland, with a limestone scar hidden in trees up to the left. *Eventually we reach the far end, where the wall turns right. Follow it to a stile into the woods, from where a path climbs to a stile by a gate. Once back into daylight, follow the wall on the left again, through another field completely surrounded by woodland. A stile at the far end deposits us into Cockshot Lane.*

Turn right along this quiet way, again enclosed by trees. This little area inland from Arnside is particularly well endowed with public footpaths, but *ignore several paths that head off into the trees until a cart track on the left signals the end of our wooded captivity. Abandon the lane in favour of the track, and it will lead unerringly to the hamlet of Haverbrack.* En route, look over the attractive tree shrouded pond to another glimpse of Ingleborough, now slotted between the nearer hills of Farleton Knott and Hutton Roof Crags. *At Haverbrack it receives a layer of tarmac before bending right to leave at a minor T-junction. Here opt for a gap-stile in the wall directly ahead, to enter the grounds of Dallam Tower.*

Set off down the field to a kissing-gate by a large iron gate onto the public road through the park, and straight across to similar gates. Bear left now, over the undulating terrain of the deer park. The slopes on the right bear distinctive 'lynchets', the cultivation terraces of Iron age times: the top of this small mound was the site of an earthwork. Ahead, the Kentmere horseshoe of fells is now prominent. *Dallam Tower itself soon appears to the left* backed by Whitbarrow Scar beyond the estuary. *The house holds the attention until a stone arched bridge appears ahead.* The river Bela provides a splendid foreground to the final view of Dallam Tower.

Cross the bridge to emerge back into the 20th century.

Bridge over the Bela, Dallam Park

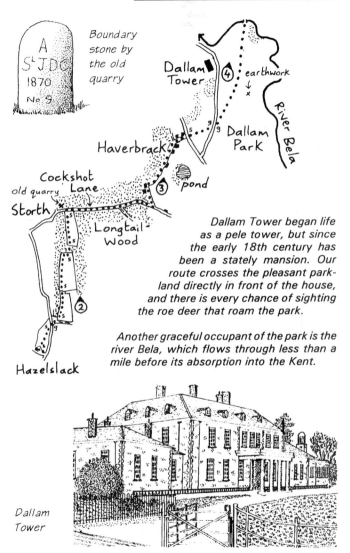

Boundary stone by the old quarry

A S⁺J.D° 1870 No 9

Dallam Tower

earthwork

River Bela

Dallam Park

Haverbrack

Cockshot Lane
old quarry
Storth

pond

Longtail Wood

Hazelslack

Dallam Tower began life as a pele tower, but since the early 18th century has been a stately mansion. Our route crosses the pleasant parkland directly in front of the house, and there is every chance of sighting the roe deer that roam the park.

Another graceful occupant of the park is the river Bela, which flows through less than a mile before its absorption into the Kent.

Dallam Tower

The bridge over the Bela leads into the B5282 Milnthorpe to Arnside road on its way out of Milnthorpe. Turn right along it for a few yards only: just after the second house on the left cross the road and head past the house and up the track. As it approaches a farmyard, leave it in favour of a more inviting green track to the right, enclosed by walls. It heads gradually uphill, but when it drops to the right take a gap-stile into the right hand of the two fields ahead. Go up by a hedge to the top, and from the gate head over to the nearest house on the right.

This modest height is a superb viewpoint, looking over the estuary. On view are Arnside Knott, Grange over Sands, Hampsfell, Newton Fell, Whitbarrow Scar, Bowfell and the Langdale Pikes, the Lyth Valley, Fairfield, Saint Sunday Crag, Caudale Moor, Ill Bell, High Street (with Whitbarrow beneath it, and Heversham church tower beneath that), Harter Fell, south to the Bowland moors with Ward's Stone in the centre and Clougha Pike prominent on the right edge, and east to the western fells of the Yorkshire Dales.

From a stile in the wall there, drop down right to emerge onto the A6. Turn left along this busy highway, which thankfully possesses a footpath. Just before the Heversham turning we cross the long defunct branch line from the main West Coast route to the Furness line, joining it at Arnside. On reaching Heversham, keep right to tramp the length of the village on a much quieter lane. Passed almost at once is Dallam School, founded in 1589.

Heversham village

Heversham has little in common with Milnthorpe, being smaller and much quieter with the main road long having avoided the village. It is routed along a parallel course to the west, for a mile during which Heversham clings to its old highway, with little depth. At the centre stands the church, Post office, and just down on the main road, the Blue Bell *inn. The imposing church of St Peter dates from 1601 and occupies a historically important site. Inside the porch is an intricately carved 8th century Anglian cross, while outside on the road is an old water pump serving St. Mary's Well.*

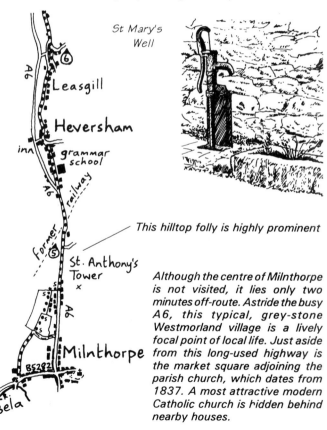

St Mary's Well

This hilltop folly is highly prominent

Although the centre of Milnthorpe is not visited, it lies only two minutes off-route. Astride the busy A6, this typical, grey-stone Westmorland village is a lively focal point of local life. Just aside from this long-used highway is the market square adjoining the parish church, which dates from 1837. A most attractive modern Catholic church is hidden behind nearby houses.

The main road is kept at arm's-length, our way being on a rise that affords views over the Lyth Valley, with the spire of Levens church conspicuous in front. Bowfell has been joined by its partner Crinkle Crags on the Lakeland skyline, while the Coniston group has also appeared. **After a mile the A6 is rejoined for a short distance to Levens Bridge.** The last stretch enjoys a good prospect of much of Levens Hall over its high wall, with the topiary garden prominent.

Cross Levens Bridge and leave the road by a stile on the right. A sketchy way heads off through Levens Park, keeping well above the river Kent. The Kent performs its swansong in Levens Park, for having spent much time among mountains, it bows out in style through this delectable parkland. The park is also graced by a shy herd of rare black Fallow deer and by Bagot goats. On leaving the park, the Kent is bridged for the last time, outside the hall. The park was laid out by Monsieur Beaumont between 1694 and 1710.

Levens Hall dates from the 13th century, since when the defensive pele tower was substantially added to in Elizabethan times. It was owned by the de Redman family for six centuries, and is now open to the paying public by the current owners, the Bagot family. Despite the great age and interest of the house, Levens' most famous feature is in its grounds: the nationally renowned topiary gardens were created in 1692, and are impeccably maintained. Also to be seen are working model steam engines, while traction engines are in steam on Sundays.

Levens Hall

Very soon we are deflected left up from the winding river, as a series of waymarks see the faint green path off through the archetypal parkland. Approaching a wood at the end, a sign sends us up to the left before the deer sanctuary, to find a stile in the wall above. Turn right down the field-side outside the wood, and from a stile in the bottom corner cross the field to the buildings of Park Head. Turn left along the winding Force Lane to rise back to the A6. Cross this dual carriageway and head up the lane opposite. At a triangular green keep right, and head along to a row of cottages at Sizergh. The rear of the Strickland Arms *is just down to the right, outside the main entrance to Sizergh Castle.*

Head up the track towards the cottages, but when it swings left, keep straight on through two stiles ahead, and rise up the wall-side outside a wood. At a stile at the top, Sizergh Castle looms impressively along to the right. Go through the stile by the gate just to the right, and make a bee-line along the wall-side to emerge in the car park.

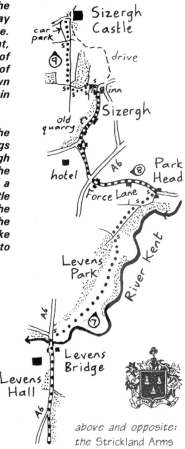

above and opposite:
the Strickland Arms

21

Sizergh Castle is a grand old house, probably the finest in old Westmorland. The oldest part is the ubiquitous pele tower, which dates from the mid-fourteenth century. Again like Levens, it was much added to in Elizabethan times, with its Great Hall being especially noteworthy. The house contains an impressive array of treasures, and has been occupied by the Stricklands for more than an astonishing 750 years. While this venerable family remain here to this day, the house was donated into the care of the National Trust in 1950, and along with its attractive grounds, is open to the public.

Sizergh Castle, featuring the pele tower on the left

Cross to the far end of the car park to a gateway in the wall opposite, and turn away from the castle environs on an enclosed cart track. Emerging at the end into a sweeping green pasture, the track runs along the wall-side across the bottom. At the far end is a stile onto a lane, though without joining it, our route turns immediately back up through a gate, and commences a pathless advance up the vast slope, thereby completing two sides of a triangle around the tight-packed wooded island.

A faint path materialises as a broad spur forms: play safe by keeping to the right of the scrub that also begins to form. In retrospect, note the impressive look of the castle before it disappears, backed by Ingleborough. Also on offer are the Yorkshire Dales mountains of Gragareth, Great Coum, Middleton Fell, Baugh Fell and the very prominent Howgill Fells above Oxenholme. To the south, a great sweep of the Kent estuary is revealed, leading out to Morecambe Bay: Arnside, its Knott and its viaduct are all conspicuous.

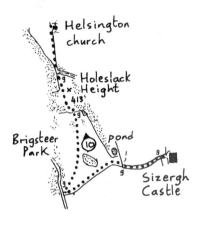

Bear up to a fence, just short of a corner to the right. Our objective is a gate a short way to the right of a step-stile. From the gate all is clear as a stony way surmounts a small brow to escape the foliage and run faintly along a green edge. There is now an outstanding panorama taking shape. *A gate at the end leads onto a farm drive, with Helsington church just a few minutes further on.*

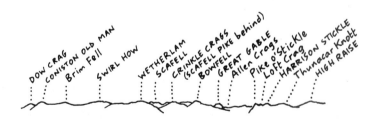

The Lakeland Fells from Helsington church

The lonely church of St John, Helsington, marks the highest point reached on this opening day - it can safely be said therefore that this is the nearest we'll come (hopefully!) to our maker today. Built in 1726 and much restored, its surround of trees afford valuable protection from the elements - the rough-cast exterior also serves this purpose. Though Helsington is the parish, the only village therein is Brigsteer. The tiny building alongside is the old school.

St John's, Helsington

The wonderfully sited seat outside Helsington church bears the words - In memory of Robert Wilkinson, who tended the gardens of Sizergh Castle for 50 years 1896-1946. *Just to the north, the limestone scars marking the start of Scout Scar impress greatly, but the view over the Lyth Valley is really something.*

After a pleasant break, strike off the track in a north-westerly direction for Brigsteer. The diagonal descent of this wide open pasture leads to a stile into the woods, from where a super path slopes down to join a cart track. Turn right along it to emerge onto a lane. Brigsteer is down to the left, though here we have two options. The onward route, introduced since the first edition of this guide, cuts out a section of road walking beyond Brigsteer. The only snag is, it cuts out Brigsteer too. So its down the road into Brigsteer for refreshment or accommodation, then either remain on the road to rejoin the route at Tullythwaite Hall, or re-ascend to this point to resume.

Even if only skirting Brigsteer, one can readily appreciate what an attractive place it is, with a large number of whitewashed cottages huddled in somewhat haphazard fashion - the Wheatsheaf *inn* plays its part in this scene. In this near-idyllic setting it shelters beneath the steeply climbing slopes leading to Scout Scar, whilst it also looks west over the Lyth Valley, to which it belongs.

below:
A corner
of Brigsteer

Fifty yards uphill is a sharp bend, just above which a broad driveway heads off into the trees on the left over a cattle-grid. This leads all the way to Barrowfield Farm, but our way there is much finer, for part-way along, just before a cattle-grid out of the trees, a waymark sends a thin path left into the trees of Honeybee Wood. At this point also note the magnificent limestone tiers of Scout Scar up above. By the way, we're also now in the Lake District National Park. Apart from five miles around Cartmel and one at Greenodd, the Way remains within its bounds to the very end.

The path runs on through the wood in cracking fashion. With wild garlic in abundance, bluebells too, and echoing with spring birdsong, this is all a far cry from the dusty drive. *Ignore any lesser branches until, with a wall ahead, the path is deflected up to the right to rejoin the drive. Barrowfield Farm is just ahead now, so advance to it and leave by an invisible path descending the field immediately below the house itself.*

Down in a little hollow a stile admits to more woodland. The narrow path descends through a carpet of wild garlic to a stile at the bottom. Cross the lush island field back into trees - meeting the first traditional Lakeland stile - *and the path heads off again to slant down to meet the terminus of a forest road. Continue the few yards to its demise, then bear left on a footpath heading away through a broad break in the trees. Advancing through colourful, semi-open terrain, the path shortly turns left back into denser plantation, but equally quickly winds down to the right to reach a gate. Emerging from the wood, bear slightly left across the field twixt gorse and rocky outcrops so typical of this area, to meet a faint green way just left of the walled paddock of Hollin Crag and Hollinwood. Turning right, the track becomes more solid to lead past the houses and out along the drive onto the narrow Garth Row Lane.*

Go left a matter of yards, then as the lane swings left, enter the field on the right by a stile by a gate beneath an island barn. Follow the left-hand wall up to the corner (past a gate) to find a slate stile. Go left with the wall and then down the field-side. The scattered settlements of the Underbarrow district are spread all about: wonderful country. *At the bottom corner a hand-gate admits to a small enclosure, and while the private gate down to the right is more obvious, go further to its left to find a crumbling wall-stile in front of a farm building. Advance a few yards through the trees then swing right, a thin path sharing a watercourse down this cramped enclosure to a gate onto a road.*

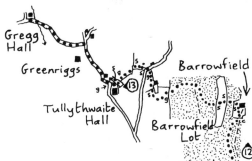

With Tullythwaite Hall just to the left, turn right for a peaceful lane section. Unless choosing to end the day at Underbarrow (in which case keep straight on) turn left at junctions at both Greenriggs and Gregg Hall. Just before the second of these, Underbarrow Beck is crossed in a lovely corner.

Barrowfield Farm

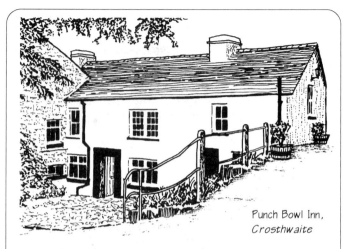

Punch Bowl Inn,
Crosthwaite

Crosthwaite is a tiny community stretching over a mile along its minor road. Comprising mainly of scattered farms and cottages, the centre can be said to be the cluster where the Punch Bowl inn and church co-habit - this is still referred to as Churchtown. The solidly built church of St. Mary's is but a century old. An attractive Post office sits further along the road, while the old corn mill is passed early in the next stage. Retaining some original features, it is currently a guest house.

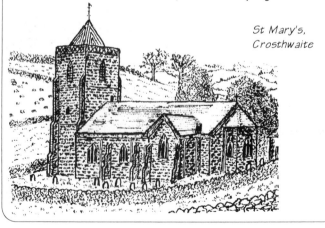

St Mary's,
Crosthwaite

The road joined at Gregg Hall is a little busier than the last, but we shall be leaving it within half a mile now. This point comes where an angled squeezer-stile is found on the right at a bend. Go up the wall-side to locate a corner-stile, then advance up to a gate. Don't use it, but take the stile a few yards along to the right. Rise up again with the wall, bearing left with it at the top to pass a few tiny outcrops. This knoll is a grand spot for a final linger, with Scout Scar extended across the skyline back over the Lyth Valley, and the currently less impressive Whitbarrow much nearer to hand.

Underbarrow inn

Underbarrow Beck

Blakebank

Crosthwaite

inn 15

14

Gregg Hall

Advance to enter the yard - or garden - of Middle Blakebank, and pass along the front to follow its drive out onto Broom Lane. Go left a short way, then at a sharp bend left take a gate in front. Head over the brow and along to the far end of the field, where a stile on the right admits onto a cart track. Turn left, improving with a grassy central strip to reach a most attractive corner with whitewashed cottages and well tended gardens. Their little road descends back onto the road, with Crosthwaite now just minutes along to the right. Lyth Gallery is 100 yards back along the road.

At the old corn mill, Crosthwaite

29

SECTION 2

—— CROSTHWAITE TO CARTMEL ——

13 miles   1700 feet of ascent

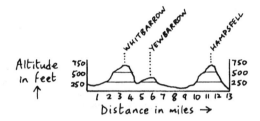

This is very much a day of ups and downs. The two high spots are the classic limestone fells of Whitbarrow and Hampsfell, which both display a profusion of outcrops and scars. Between these breezy heights the Way takes in a corner of the scattered settlement of Witherslack and the charming Winster Valley, along with corners of Newton Fell and Lindale village. All of these relatively minor heights are excellent viewpoints.

The memorial cairn,
Lord's Seat,
Whitbarrow

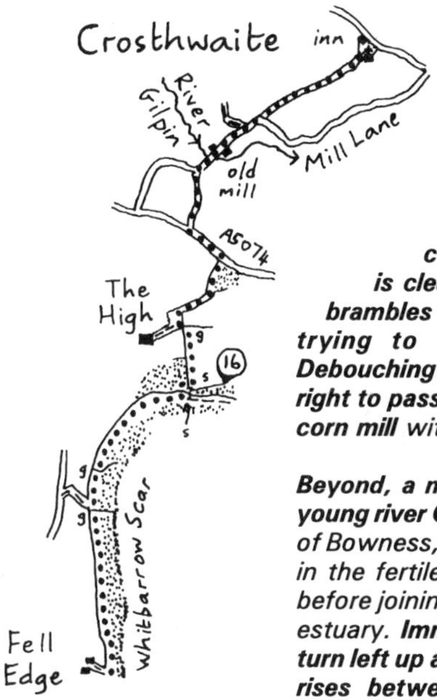

Crosthwaite

From the inn go down the track to the church. A wicket-gate adjacent to the tower leads onto a delightful grassy by-way running down to the overflow church-yard. Just beyond this point it narrows quite considerably, and though it is clearly maintained, the keen brambles might nevertheless prove trying to those with bare legs! Debouching onto leafy Mill Lane, turn right to pass the restored Crosthwaite corn mill with its mill race still intact.

Beyond, a modest bridge crosses the young river Gilpin. The Gilpin rises east of Bowness, and spends most of its life in the fertile acres of the Lyth Valley before joining the Kent just short of its estuary. Immediately over the bridge, turn left up an inviting green way. This rises between hedgerows onto the normally quiet A5074. Go left just 150 yards and turn up the drive that climbs towards The High.

Just as it swings right for the farm (above a former limekiln), break off to pass through the upper of two gates over to the left. Climb the field-side to a stile in the top corner. Before entering, pause to survey the wide prospect. Far beyond scattered Crosthwaite - with its church prominent - are the Coniston Fells and Bowfell and company: slotting neatly between Lord's Lot and Scout Scar is the Whinfell ridge, above the Lune Gorge. In the wood (rich with a remarkable springtime carpet of wild garlic and bluebells) a thin path climbs to a wall-stile to emerge onto a cart-track. Follow this to the right, descending rather roughly at first but quickly easing out in all ways to mature into a super green way. With fields below and the tree-clad lower slopes of Whitbarrow above, the buildings of Fell Edge soon appear below. This attractive farmstead has lost much appeal since the unfortunate demise of the house.

31

Whitbarrow is an immense plateau-like upland covering many square miles between the Lyth and Winster Valleys. Despite its summit reaching a mere 706 feet, there is a great feeling of space here, and one could wander all day and not discover half of its secrets - one could easily get lost too! It is a major landmark in south Lakeland, being recognisable from all directions. The main feature is a near five mile long scar that decorates the western and southern edges of the fell.

If the sun shines here then the brilliant white of the limestone is remarkably dazzling, from the near vertical scar to the profuse pavements and rocks liberally scattered across the plateau. The summit, named Lord's Seat, is surmounted by a noble cairn that bears a tablet commemorating the late Canon Hervey, a founder of the Lake District Naturalist's Trust.

The complete panorama is possibly the finest to be had, a bold claim perhaps. but it rather splendid. From the south-east there is a long sweep of Bowland moors from Clougha Pike to Ward's Stone, then the Dales mountains of Ingleborough, Gragareth, Great Coum, Casterton Fell, Middleton Fell, Baugh Fell, the Howgill Fells, and round to the Whinfell ridge and a full line-up of Lakeland Fells (see also overleaf).

In addition, nearer to hand are Newton Fell, Heysham power station, the Kent estuary, Arnside and its viaduct under the Knott, Farleton Fell, the Lyth Valley below Scout Scar, with the whitewashed houses of Brigsteer prominent. Also, of course, there is a vast spread of Whitbarrow itself on parade, with limestone scars spread across the plateau in abundance and richly wooded flanks rolling away.

The erratic boulder, Flodder Allotment

Shortly after Fell Edge, the path forsakes its level course and heads up into the trees. Slanting across the rough fellside it negotiates a pronounced gap in the limestone scar. Halt again to enjoy a superb retrospective view over the Winster Valley that makes the puffing and panting worthwhile. *Advancing, a thin trod runs on to a stile in the wall a little further back: strictly speaking, our footpath bears further right to a second stile further along the wall. Turn right over the wall until it bends away to the right. The objective now is Lord's Seat, highest point on Whitbarrow.*

From the wall corner bear slightly left up the gentle slope, a thin trod making for a conspicuous large boulder. On arrival it proves to be two not one, though clearly it once was only one! It is also erratic, that is, it was deposited here by glacier amidst a landscape alien to them. *Maintain the direction to a large cairn a little further. From here the summit cairn is visible, still some way off.*

A natural looking ditch can then be followed to the left, the path taking advantage of it as it winds round beneath a rash of stones crowned by a large pillar. The path peters out to approach a solid wall running across the fell. Go left with it a short way to reach a stile and gate at a wall-corner. These bear the logo of the Cumbria Wildlife Trust, formerly the Lake District Naturalist's Trust. Here we enter the Hervey Nature Reserve, which occupies Flodder Allotment on the highest reaches of the fell, 250 acres.

A good path heads away from the stile through a surround of attractive silver birch, until interrupted by a long, low limestone scar. This deflects the path away from the attendant wall and steadily up to gain the summit cairn.

From the cairn on Lord's Seat head west to another soundly built cairn, and maintain that direction on an excellent cairned path negotiating an assortment of outcrops (both plant and rock). On approaching the grassy edge of the fell ensure the brakes are applied early, as a descent from this point would be one's last. Having marvelled at both the scar itself, and also the thorough carpet of woodland (it still wouldn't cushion a fall), note also the towers of Witherslack Hall pushing through the trees. *Turn left along the edge, still on terrain 'par excellence' until the path drops slightly to leave the top at a stile marked by another CWT sign.*

A step descent through the trees (treading cautiously with a full pack) is followed by a short stroll to the edge of the wood. Here, bear right off the track through a gateway, then immediately left along the edge of a sports field to a stile. Turn right on the pathway which runs along to a gate by some barns. Here pause to look back at the finest of Whitbarrow's cliffs, Chapel Head Scar. This is a very popular rock climbing ground where some of the toughest grades are challenged: negotiated agreements permit the birds of the cliffs to nest in peace before the antics begin.

From the gate a short-lived rough lane climbs to a road. turn right just as far as Witherslack Hall Farm. The hall itself was built in 1874 as a hunting lodge for Lord Derby - the arms are borne on Witherslack's distant inn - and is a special school. *Then turn up a broad rough track to the left. On emerging from wooded enclosure by two enviably sited houses, cross the field to a gate in the far corner, and continue along a good track through woodland. The trees slowly relent, and when the wall turns off to the left the track falters: bear half-right to pick up another green trackway which leads to a stile by a gate in the wall opposite.* This vast pasture we are leaving is a lovely limestone based reach, part of one of the lowest yet loveliest fells imaginable, Yewbarrow.

A good path heads away from the stile through yet more delightful woodland. After a while it descends a little steeply, and when the slope curtails take a path branching off to the right at a cairn. This zigzags quickly down to join a quiet lane, with Witherslack church just across to the right.

Looking back to Chapel Head Scar

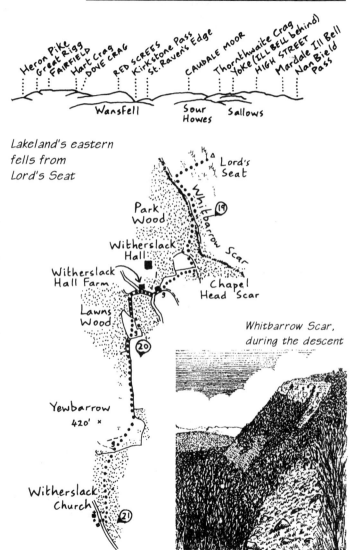

Heron Pike
Great Rigg
FAIRFIELD
Hart Crag
DOVE CRAG
RED SCREES
Kirkstone Pass
St. Raven's Edge
CAUDALE MOOR
Thornthwaite Crag
Yoke (ILL BELL behind)
HIGH STREET
Mardale Ill Bell
Nan Bield Pass

Wansfell   Sour Howes   Sallows

Lakeland's eastern
fells from
Lord's Seat

Lord's Seat

Whitbarrow Scar

Park Wood

19

Witherslack Hall

Witherslack Hall Farm

Chapel Head Scar

9

Lawns Wood

20

Yewbarrow
420' ×

9

Witherslack Church

21

_Whitbarrow Scar,
during the descent_

Witherlack's modest little church was erected in 1669, and stands by an attractive green. Alongside in this entirely lovely corner are the former schoolhouse (Dean Barwick's school and masters house, rebuilt 1874, though founded in 1678) and the former vicarage, now a country house hotel where morning coffee and afternoon tea might be obtained. Note also the Victorian letterbox and the old coach house.

St Paul's,
Witherslack

Though many villages in these parts are spread out, Witherslack appears scattered to the four corners of the earth. Our route passes the hall and church, but Witherslack also hides the hamlets of Beck Head, Mill Side and Town End. An inn stands even further afield on a sidelined section of the old A590.

Leave the green by a signposted path through the car park behind the hotel. Our path is waymarked down to the right, passing through an orchard left of a tennis court and down into woodland. It swings to the left and then shortly turns down through an old iron gate and a few steps onto a lane at Blea Crag. Cross straight over and head off on a track behind the houses, only to leave it there by a broad path forking right into the trees. Beyond an old stile it advances to the edge of the wood. Aiming for the gate on the left, do not go through it but follow the wall heading away. A clear path is picked up to descend to the right through more trees. From a wall-

stile at the bottom go round to the right of the buildings. A gate admits to a short drive that leads out onto a minor lane opposite the farm of Slate Hill. A level stretch of the Winster Valley now ensues, with colourful Newton Fell to our right.

The river Winster rises south of Bowness on Windermere, but shuns publicity by heading further south to form a beautiful, richly wooded dale. The river witnesses little of man's work, for only the tiny hamlet of Bowland Bridge graces its banks. The Winster retains its own identity throughout its fourteen mile journey from source to sea. It empties into Morecambe Bay, and the traditional Lancashire-Westmorland boundary follows it virtually all the way.

Turn left to a T-junction then fork right, the lane being very slow to ease itself into a rougher surface. Shortly beyond this point is a fork: the main way bears right, through a gate into Nichols Wood. As the drive to Nichols Wood Farm it undulates through this pleasant woodland to reach the farmstead. Keep left of all buildings and out into a field, where a green trackway runs outside a wood to reach a farm bridge on the river Winster.

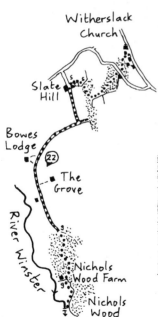

The Grove

Cross the bridge and turn downstream only as far as the first old hedge on the right. Skirt two sides of the field to a gate in the opposite corner, and keep on the field-side to the far corner. Here a short-lived enclosed way takes up the going, and at the new triangular plantation at the end, bear left to a gate into the colourful country of Wilson Hills. This area of rock outcrops and rough pasture has had a hard time of it, being split by the Lindale by-pass and the scene of unsightly excavations.

Advance a few yards to a broad track, and turn right along it. Shortly after, it turns down to the right, where a stile by a pylon sees escape into a field. Across it are a few rock outcrops with a long spread of woodland behind: bear left with the pylons to a narrowing corner with a set of pens behind. A stile on the right sees a few yards of ungainly posturing all to avoid crossing the pens, then gaining a broad enclosed track to rise onto a lane. Turn right along it for 100 yards then take a stile over the wall on the left to gain the foot of Newton Fell.

Open fellside is immediately gained, and a few minutes of potential rough going are now on the cards. The well worn path slanting right is bound for the climbers' training ground on the prominent slab of Lindale Crag. *Our way is a thinner trod running up to the left. It rises through undergrowth to falter on a minor plateau. The objective is a ladder-stile in a wall descending the fell, but the slim path to it is difficult to locate in choking bracken. with luck it will be found, and makes life so much easier: remember not to gain too much height on this steep fellside. From the stile all is plain sailing. Slant immediately up again on a clearer path through easy ground, and at the next wall simply rise up with it until reaching a stile.*

This is a grand spot to linger, this southern outpost of Newton Fell being particularly well positioned for looking back over the first two stages of the Way: Whitbarrow, the Kent estuary and the Bay, and Arnside Knott are all well displayed. Ingleborough's now familiar outline is located in the middle of the adjacent pylon! While Newton Fell runs further north for several miles, our route traces its southerly fall to Lindale. Once happily connected with the village, it is now savagely severed by the huge sweep of the by-pass.

Lindale by-pass from Newton Fell

THE RIVER WINSTER TO LINDALE

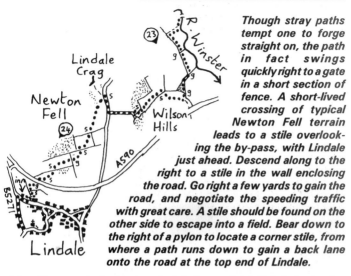

Though stray paths tempt one to forge straight on, the path in fact swings quickly right to a gate in a short section of fence. A short-lived crossing of typical Newton Fell terrain leads to a stile overlooking the by-pass, with Lindale just ahead. Descend along to the right to a stile in the wall enclosing the road. Go right a few yards to gain the road, and negotiate the speeding traffic with great care. A stile should be found on the other side to escape into a field. Bear down to the right of a pylon to locate a corner stile, from where a path runs down to gain a back lane onto the road at the top end of Lindale.

The village centre is down to the left, but maintain height by turning up the few yards to the Royal Oak inn. At the junction here turn along to the left, as far as a lane down into the village (see next page). Just yards past it turn up a cul-de-sac of modern housing.

St. Paul's, Lindale

Lindale reveals many attractive corners to those tempted by a detour down into its centre, where there is also another inn. Like any village similarly freed, Lindale has fallen back into more peaceful times since the heavy traffic left its streets. However, a local man was making his name in the world of transport long before congested roads were known. Thomas Wilkinson, dubbed the 'ironmaster', was instrumental in the creation of the world's first iron bridge, at Coalbrookdale in Shropshire. He also experimented with iron ships, first sailing a model in the Winster. He died in 1808, and is buried in the village church. If returning to the route by the winding back lane, then St Paul's parish church will be passed. With its puny tower it was built in 1828 (with later additions), and sits in a hollow far beneath the road: George Fox preached on the site in 1652.

At 727 feet, Hampsfell narrowly overtops the day's previous summit on Whitbarrow. Its full title of Hampsfield Fell is seldom used other than on OS maps. A broad ridge, gifted with limestone in profusion and superb views, this fell is a real gem. The hospice is a solid stone structure erected in 1835 by George Remington, a Cartmel pastor, for the use of weary travellers. The attractions on the viewing platform include a view indicator, and the panorama includes Black Combe, a sweeping seascape that takes in most of the Furness coastline, Snaefell (Isle of Man), Blackpool Tower, Heysham, the Bowland moors, Arnside Knott,

 Ingleborough, Whernside, Howgill Fells, Shap Fells, and then a very full Lakeland fells skyline. Within the shelter is a fireplace, and all around the walls is a remarkable screed. One can at least read this, whatever the visibility!

The Hospice, Hampsfell

At the head of the cul-de-sac (Lingarth) one is back in the country. A rough track is crossed to a gap-stile, and a steep field climbed to a wicket-gate into woodland. Cross straight over a private drive and drop down to another such gate. Cross the field to a gate up the opposite slope, and rise up to the reach the tarmac drive serving Home Farm, Hampsfield.

At once leave the surfaced drive by way of a rough track behind the house on the left. It peters out in a field but a stile on the left rekindles a path through grand woodland to reach a gap-stile. Gaining the foot of Hampsfell's upper slopes, a good track follows the wall on the left to an intervening stile. Continue in such fine fettle as far as a stile on the left out of Eggerslack Wood. Here turn right up a zigzag path into a modest limestone amphitheatre.

Bear up to the left to gain a stile in the rising wall. Follow the wall up on a path that continues beyond the wall-corner to quickly gain the hospice on the summit of the fell. A massive pile of stones, probably a burial cairn, precedes the hospice. While the modern yellow posts may keep people on the right track, they do little for the essence of the place.

The Royal Oak, Lindale

41

For a village this size, Cartmel boasts bags of character. It has a unique independence, owed partly to its lively past but also to its geographical location. Formerly in Lancashire but not in Furness, then part of all-embracing Cumbria. The Priory church of St. Mary and St. Michael was founded in 1188 for Augustinian canons, and it survived the dissolution due to its parish church status. Restored in the early 1600s, the priory has a most sparsely decorated interior in which lies much of its charm. Having said that, the choir stalls and the oak screen are truly magnificent. Also of interest is the well preserved Harrington tomb, over 600 years old.

There is much further interest here too, including the racecourse and gatehouse. The former boasts surely the most attractive setting of any, though only sees action on Spring and August Bank holidays. On these weekends Cartmel is a riot of colour and activity, with a funfair, stalls and such like filling the centre of the ground - a lively occasion best avoided if seeking accommodation at the same time! The 14th century gatehouse was fortified to defend the priory, and still bridges the road into the square. It is in the care of the National Trust and open for viewing. Four inns and numerous interesting shops add further to the delights of Cartmel.

Cartmel Priory

From the hospice do not consider a bee-line for Cartmel, but take the path due south to a well-built cairn on a limestone ledge. Continue to a gap-stile in the wall below, and remain on this broad path through a long collapsed wall, bearing right at a fork as far as a marked depression. Without advancing up the minor brow ahead, turn on the path to the right. This makes an accomplished, direct descent of the fell to a gate onto farmland. Descend the wall-side to a gate at the bottom, then aim directly across the field for Pit Farm.

Go to the right of all the buildings to find a kissing-gate, then bear left towards the first of the more traditional buildings. Here a wall-stile is found by a sign good enough for a road junction. Follow the fence across the rise of the field, Cartmel re-appearing only minutes ahead. From a gate at the end a short snicket debouches onto a lane on the edge of the village. Go left and then sharp right on Priest Lane to reach a gate into the churchyard. Skirt round the priory - a must for a visit - and out the other side to enter the main street as it opens out into the village square.

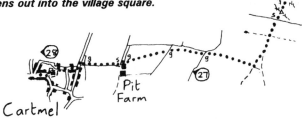

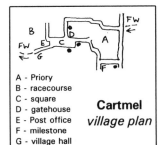

A - Priory
B - racecourse
C - square
D - gatehouse
E - Post office
F - milestone
G - village hall
● - inns

Cartmel
village plan

In Cartmel

43

SECTION 3

——— CARTMEL TO LOWICK ———

12½ miles   1150 feet of ascent

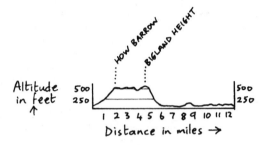

The walk from Cartmel to Lowick is one of two distinct halves. Firstly a broad, undulating ridge high above the Leven estuary is traversed from Howbarrow to Bigland Tarn, then a descent to valley levels heralds a complete change of environment. The river Leven is accompanied to Greenodd, from where the Way strikes inland to follow the well wooded valley of the river Crake through several unassuming villages to Lowick.

The Farmers Arms, *Lowick*

_Leave the village square by the lane to the left of the Post office
to enter the racecourse. Incidentally, if you should be here on
racing weekends, fear not, for access across the track is only
denied for the few minutes when the horses are actually in full
flight. On crossing the track bear half-right to the other side, where
re-cross to find a kissing-gate into Park Wood. A path climbs
through this most outstanding of bluebell woods. Ignoring any
branches, it soon levels out to leave the trees by a narrow gap-stile
into a field. Follow the wall away to emerge onto a lane. Go left
along this quiet road, which will lead eventually_ - including a climb
past an attractive old mill dam - _to the demise of its surface at
Howbarrow farm._

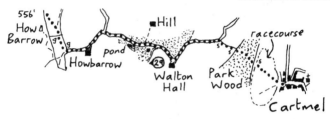

_Do not enter the yard, but follow the track (an old road) through a
gate on the right to climb past the buildings._ At the brow of the hill
the Leven estuary makes its first appearance, with the Leven
Viaduct prominent, as is Ulverston watched over by the monument
on Hoad Hill. Just ahead is the sturdy little height of How Barrow.
Unfortunately there is no right of way to this fine viewpoint. It is
not quite the highest point of the Ellerside ridge to which it belongs,
but its rocky knoll surmounted by an OS column certainly deserves
that honour. The Ellerside
ridge runs from north to
south, separating the
Cartmel Valley from the
Leven Valley and estuary.

_The approach to
Howbarrow Farm_

From the gate at the end of the lane, turn right on the green track. This climbs the field on the near side of How Barrow. Through a gate in a fence remain on the main track bearing left, which - a little faintly in parts - runs on to the far end of the enclosure. Midway, at a knoll, a super view over the estuary opens out.

From the gate the track fades somewhat, but picks up on passing a tilted rock slab larger than its fellow outcrops. All these tilted slabs scattered about the ridge are formed of Silurian slate, which features regularly in various corners of High Furness. From the gate in the next wall a surround of thistles is slowly joined by bracken, with a lovely wood on the right. The

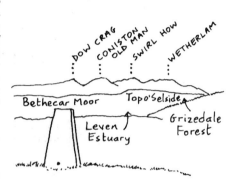

Looking north along the How Barrow ridge to the next two stages of the Way

path bears right to join a wall, which remains in close attendance until the ridge narrows to offer its best views yet. This adds the steep plunge of the Stribers woods and the marsh and woodland of Roudsea to the features already on offer. Greenodd waits patiently across the estuary.

Just beyond here, a gate is reached at the edge of Collkield Wood. Though the path continues through it to join the route in the next enclosure, this short linking section is not designated a right of way. *Those of us with a conscience will, therefore, engage in a modest detour by taking a stile in the wall on the right. Cross the pathless field, curving right as it drops away, to pass through an old wall and continue on with marsh on the left, crumbling wall on the right. At the end a rough track is joined, and this leads left along to Speel Bank.*

Head through the yard, beyond which the road becomes surfaced. Leave it at once by a gate in the fence on the left, and rise with the wall. When this swings away, go left to find a gate into a plantation.

A good path heads through the trees to soon emerge at the far side. A large tract of rough pasture (the eastern part of Stribers Allotment) is entered, with a bewildering choice of tracks.

Advance a few yards to the first track and go right. Ignoring lesser diversions, remain on this as it makes its way across to the far side. Approaching a wall there, bear right with it, only descending a little before reaching a gate in it. A faint way heads away right to a gate in a fence (note the marshy pool on the left) from which bear left between outcrops to espy the lone dwelling of Grassgarth below, backed by High Stribers Wood. The track descends in that direction, slanting a little left to a gate onto a lane. Turn right, then double back on the drive to Grassgarth.

Tracing the Way north on the Ellerside ridge

47

Pass along the left side of the house at Grassgarth to a private looking gate (with another just behind, to the left) into the field behind. A brief view over the estuary reveals the Hoad Hill monument now breaking the skyline above Ulverston. *At the far end a gate leads into High Stribers Wood.*

A grand path climbs through the trees. Leaving the wood at another gate, it emerges into more colourful upland. There is now a grand view over the estuary from Greenodd downwards, and also back over the Ellerside ridge. *The green trackway curves around to the left, then advances over this easy terrain to find Bigland Tarn sat beneath us. A more solid track descends towards it, its bank making a suitable five minute halt.* Seen ahead is Bigland Hall, which dates from the early 19th century. It currently operates as a sporting estate, with riding and fishing included.

On approaching the outflow of the tarn, bear left to commence a long and direct descent on an improving path. Ignore any branches as the path steepens with the stream on the right to enter Bigland Woods. The only break between the gate and the valley bottom comes on encountering a green track through a very broad break: cross straight over to regain our path, which now meanders about a little before making a concerted descent to the road.

Turn along to the right, but make an early detour along a lane branching right to pass through the interesting old hamlet of Low Wood. A left turn after the last building at Low Wood leads back to the main road at Low Wood Bridge.

Bigland Tarn

Low Wood is a tiny settlement, centrepiece of which is the Clock Tower, part of a splendid building that once housed a gunpowder works. These operated throughout the 19th century and into the beginning of the 20th century. Today it is the base for local crafts, featuring a crystal engraver.

The Clock Tower
Low Wood

Haverthwaite

Leven

Low Wood

Bigland Hall

Bigland Tarn

Bigland Woods

(33)

Bigland Heights

Grassgarth Heights

High Stribers Wood

Grassgarth

49

As the outflow from Windermere, England's largest lake, the Leven is a ready made river of substantial proportions. Its journey to form one of the main inlets of Morecambe Bay is but short. Bridged by only five roads, its final two bridges are both related to the former railway. The penultimate is an uninspiring railway bridge, while the final crossing is our impending footbridge. This costly modern structure safeguards the right of way that was 'dismantled' with the old railway viaduct.

Between Low Wood and Greenodd the Leven is a haven for birdlife, while the whole area is rich in natural history. The confines of Roudsea Wood support a wide variety of trees, thanks largely to both limestone and slate being in evidence. Deer also frequent the quiet woodland, which merges with salt marsh to create a most unusually varied wildlife habitat. A large area of peat bog is being restored by blocking drains to maintain high water levels required by the rare plants and insects. Access other than by right of way is by permit only.

Alongside
the Leven
below
Low Wood

LOW WOOD TO ROUDSEA WOOD

Do not cross Low Wood Bridge unless detouring into Haverthwaite, a few minutes along to the right. Haverthwaite is a scattered village with the Anglers Arms offering refreshment, just off route. It is better known however for its preserved steam railway. The Lakeside and Haverthwaite Railway runs where its name suggests, up the valley of the Leven to the foot of Windermere. Here one can connect with the steamers that ply the length of the lake. The railway's journey is a short but very attractive route, dominated by woodland. Trains run daily at Easter and from May to October. The branch line originally served Lakeside from the Furness Railway at Ulverston, by way of Greenodd. Haverthwaite station boasts a licensed restaurant and tearoom, open from April to December: there is also an engine shed and souvenir shop.

At Low Wood Bridge, take the driveway opposite. This now surfaced way is largely ours for some time to come, though we have an early break from it. When it swings away from the Leven take a stile in front to remain with the river. Hug its bank for three enjoyable field's lengths before being ushered back onto the drive at a bend. Follow it right past the ruinous Fish House, with the river still in close proximity. *Look back to see Bigland Woods and the Ellerside ridge.* **The drive runs on to the entrance to Roudsea Wood. After a brief lesson about this National Nature Reserve head off into the trees. The way soon re-emerges at the other side,** *with a view ahead now to the grey houses of Greenodd and Penny Bridge climbing the hillside.*

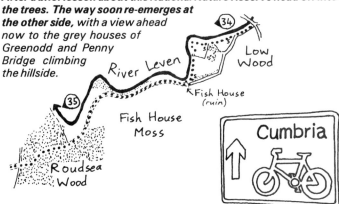

Along the drive to Roudsea Wood we must share our Way with those on the Cumbria Cycle Way, which enjoys a 260 mile journey encircling the Lake District

The drive aims directly for the houses in view, and when it turns off to the isolated marshland farm of Mearness, maintain the bee-line on a field-path that rises over a flood embankment which surprisingly does not provide the anticipated view of the river. Undaunted, continue on through one more pasture to a stile. This time an animated scene lies ahead: directly in front is a long concrete footbridge which is used to cross the Leven in style.

On reaching the thundering highway go left a short distance, then double back under the road on a path that saves us from dicing with death as we did at Lindale. It follows the hapless Crake upstream a few yards, then turns left to enter the main street of Greenodd just short of the Ship Inn.

Turning right along Greenodd's street, leave by a narrow path that climbs away just beyond the Machell Arms (and a bakery). At the drive at the top, go left to join a lane. Turn up this, passing Penny Bridge school and church to arrive at a T-junction. A right turn leads down a lane lined with houses and the Britannia inn. At the bottom of the hill cross straight over the busy A5092. This is the Furness 'by-pass' for traffic heading for the Cumberland coast. Continue down the lane to cross the Crake by Penny Bridge itself.

Still in evidence on many a Furness pub doorway

Hartleys is a famous name in this part of the world: unfortunately however, it is no longer brewed with loving care in the market town three or four miles down the road, but trunked in from the outskirts of Manchester.

The approach to the church of St. Mary the Virgin.

What's in a name? This is the parish church of Egton cum Newland, which serves the villages of Greenodd, Penny Bridge and Spark Bridge.

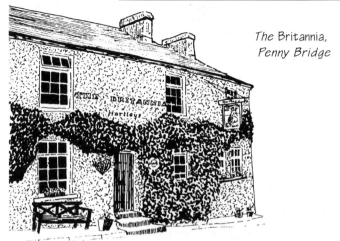

The Britannia,
Penny Bridge

Greenodd is a small village guarding the entrance to the Crake Valley, standing watch at its late confluence with the Leven. The Crake's final yards are something of an anti-climax, as its last act is to pass beneath the two great spans of the by-pass before losing its identity. Greenodd had a livelier past, having once been a thriving little port with its own railway station. Until the by-pass it also sat astride the A590 to Ulverston and Barrow. In contrast, its main street now resembles the proverbial one-horse town, having gone to the other extreme to be closed off to form a cul-de-sac. The happy result is peace and quiet for residents however, who can cross from inn to shop and back to bakery and inn in safety. This is a major turning point of our walk, for here we finally abandon our flirtations with the Bay: the next time we confront the sea it will be the real thing, in the form of the Irish Sea at Ravenglass.

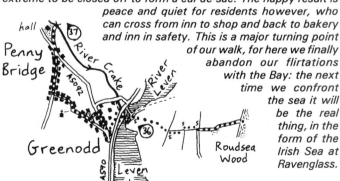

53

The river Crake runs for a mere five miles from the foot of Coniston Water to its absorption into the Leven at Greenodd. It was once a hive of activity, its banks playing host to a number of bobbin mills that served the Lancashire cotton industry. Interesting evidence abounds during our short spell in its company. Also thriving in this valley (as well as its High Furness neighbours) were iron furnaces. More usually operating on a small scale, as bloomeries, the Crake Valley had its share of larger scale furnaces. The abundance of suitable wood for charcoal burning was the reason iron ore mined from lower down the Furness peninsula was brought here for smelting.

Go left along the back road past Bridge End, enjoying fine views over the river: looking back, Penny Bridge Hall sits on a knoll above the bridge. Within a few minutes an old mill is approached. **Don't take the first drive, but the second one down to the left. This runs above a terrace of old cottages, and the mill. On the sharp bend at the end of the buildings, leave the track by a gate. Contour across the field until the wall drops away, then, in theory, slope down a little to follow an old mill-race.**

In practice, the path is overgrown and obstructed. It is easier to stick close to the field bottom to the far end. Here, don't take the obvious gap in the low descending wall, but turn into the bottom corner to find a gap, a tiny stream, and a stile into a more welcoming field. On the left here is the simple weir and the sluice gate at the start of the cut's split from the river.

Here leave the river to follow the field boundary slanting up the field. At the top corner pass through a gateway and remain with the wall on the right to reach a lane adjacent to Lane Head Farm. Turn left for a gradual descent into Spark Bridge.

Spark Bridge is a tiny, tidy village stood mainly on the west bank of the Crake. A pleasant green lies adjacent to the river, as does a bobbin mill that survived into the first edition of this guide. Dominating the village, it added a certain character to the place, though sadly it is now derelict. To add to local woes, the inn was closed and up for sale at the time of this revision: hopefully it will survive to serve ale again. Spark Bridge is a locally important junction, for lanes head away in no less than five directions to neighbouring villages.

PENNY BRIDGE TO SPARK BRIDGE

Although nearer to Spark Bridge, the Farmers Arms, *on the main road at the top of the village, belongs to Lowick, being a level walk from the Green. It is a most interestingly laid out building, boasting a spinning gallery and some round chimneys typical of larger, older houses of the district.* Parts of the inn date back to the 14th century. The map overleaf indicates its position, whilst the pub is illustrated at the start of the chapter.

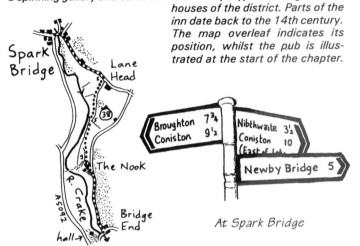

At Spark Bridge

Penny
Bridge

Leave the bridge by heading up the road towards Coniston, but soon after passing the Royal Oak *inn take a narrow lane off to the right. This soon forks, and here leave it for a snicket almost straight ahead.* Before entering it, turn to see a house renovated to incorporate a fine spinning gallery. *The snicket is interrupted briefly by a yard, but then resumes in excellent fashion,* largely between hedgerows and rampant with spring flowers, and with good views over the Crake.

Ahead, the Blawith Fells lead the eye to the Coniston Fells, which will dominate both our thoughts and our surrounds for today and beyond. *All too soon a track is joined which leads up to emerge onto the A5084 at the entrance to Lowick Green. Turn right to find the large green itself, possibly escaping the road by crossing it to the line of houses on its far side.*

Back at the main road, take a stile on the left soon after the last building. Head away to a gate, continue with the wall until the corner, then bear half-right to a stile opposite. Go round the right side of this small field to emerge onto a farmer's access lane: leave this by the left-hand of the gates along to the right. Head away with the wall on the left, and from a stile at the end, cross a large pasture (slab footbridge midway) to a gap-stile on the skyline. One more field leads to the guiding beacon of Lowick church.

A lane runs along the front of the church, and if followed down to the right it leads quickly into Lowick Bridge. This scattering of cottages is another place not geared up to tourism, though it does possess the Red Lion *inn and a bike hire centre.*

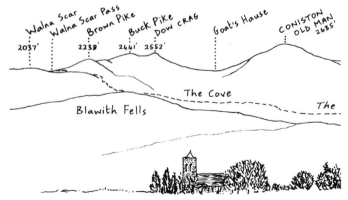

SPARK BRIDGE TO LOWICK BRIDGE

Lowick church was built around a century ago of distinctly local materials. It boasts an enviable setting looking north to the Coniston Fells, whilst its churchyard crocus display is simply unforgettable. The church evidently plays a largely impartial role in Lowick life, for its profound isolation attaches it to neither Green nor Bridge.

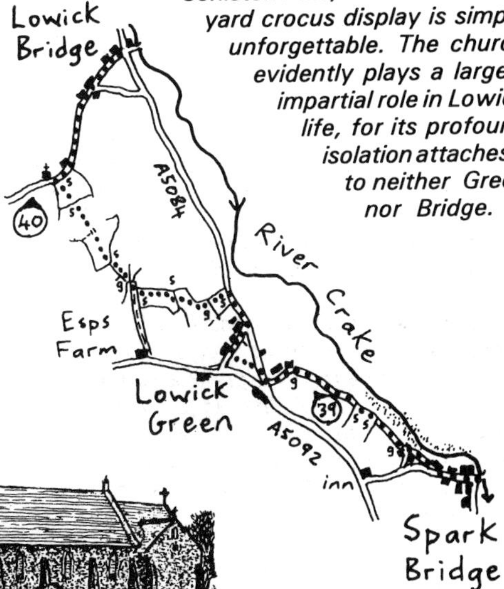

Lowick Bridge
A5084
40
River Crake
Esps Farm
Lowick Green
39
A5092
inn
Spark Bridge

St Luke's, Lowick

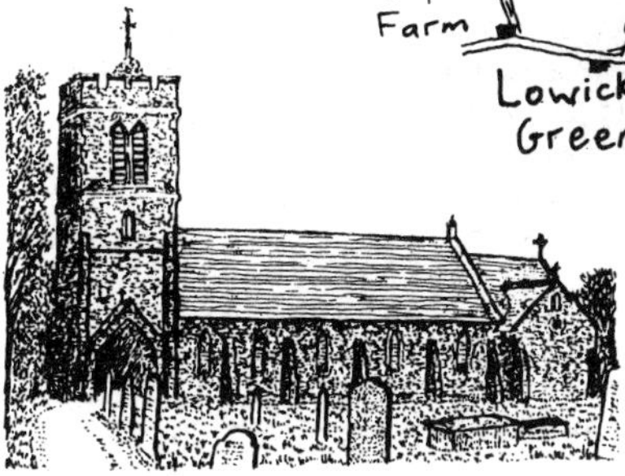

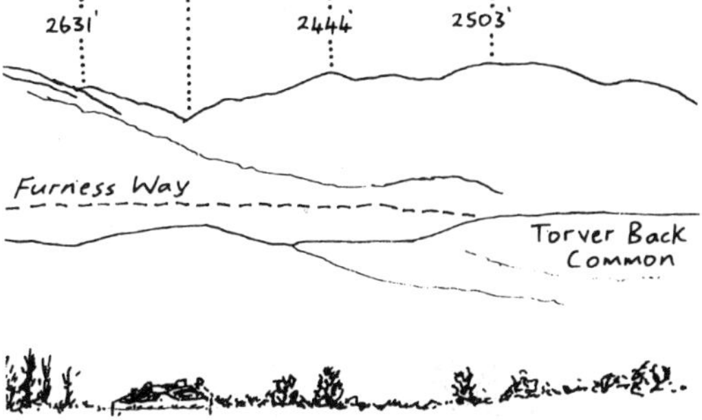

SWIRL HOW
2631'
Swirl Hause
Black Sails
2444'
WETHERLAM
2503'
Furness Way
Torver Back Common

Looking north to the Coniston Fells from Lowick Green

SECTION 4

──── LOWICK TO CONISTON ────

11 miles   1550 feet of ascent

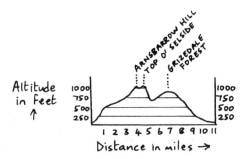

This fourth day is mostly an upland trek, high above the east side of the Crake Valley and the entire length of Coniston Water. Hill farming environs lead to Bethecar Moor and two 1000ft tops, then the extensive Grizedale Forest is entered. Eventually the head of the lake is reached and then Coniston village itself. The mighty Coniston Fells dominate the views throughout the day.

The Red Lion, Lowick Bridge

From the main road at Lowick Bridge crossroads go down to cross the bridge and take a sharp turn left. This road shadows the entire eastern shore of Coniston Water where our route rejoins it near the end of the day. We leave it, however, by the first lane on the right, signposted to Oxenpark. Bessy Bank Lane climbs steeply through trees: you may well call it something else when you get to the top, though it still might begin with 'B'. Take your time, therefore, through this lovely woodland. Shortly after the trees end the gradient eases and the drive to Hill Park is taken to the left.

Pass straight through the farmyard, then turn left after the last barn along a walled track. From here we have a fine view back down to the valley, Kirkby Moor windfarm dominant high above the neat, white-washed cottages of Lowick Bridge - with the church prominent too.

Lowick Bridge

The walled track from Hill Park swings right between hedgerows and into a field. As the track rises up, don't be tempted off to the left (gateway and then stile), but climb to a gate at the top of this narrowing field. From it remain with the wall on the right to a stile on a corner. Don't use it, but bear left away from the wall to a gate which appears ahead. This is an interesting viewpoint in that it reveals all the Crake Valley downstream and far below, but also looks promisingly ahead to the Coniston Fells. *From it, a faint green way crosses a lofty pasture to reach a gate into a wood.*

A clear green path leads through the trees and emerges into a broad walled way. A fine prospect greets the eye, nothing finer than the shapely dome of Arnsbarrow Hill, directly ahead: over to the left is a grand picture of the Blawith Fells, backed by the Dunnerdale Fells and Caw. *When the wall on the right departs, go straight on to enter the farmyard at Stock.*

Pass straight through the farmyard at Stock and out on its drive. On joining the head of Bletherbarrow Lane, turn right on the track that takes over. Through a gate, take the left branch alongside a wall, a super green track through lush sheep pasture. Passing through another gate, with a good deal of Bethecar Moor now revealed enticingly in front, the path rises round to reach the barn at Low Bethecar. Zigzag up the slope behind on a tractor-track, to gain the open moor by a stile alongside a gate. It's great to be on a real moor!

Low Bethecar

Turn left to follow the path alongside the intake wall. At an indentation is a stile, from where the right of way heads away to find High Bethecar below. Descending to the rear of the farm, it does not disturb their peace, but turns back up to the right where a short lived dry valley sees the path back onto the moor at a stile. The more logical path remains on the moor to leave the wall at the next corner, heading directly away to merge into that leaving the cultivated confines of High Bethecar.

Head along this wide green track onto Bethecar Moor. On approaching the onset of a marshy area, the diversion over Arnsbarrow Hill can be contemplated. The top should be easily identifiable as the shapeliest acclivity in the vicinity, with Top o'Selside set further back, to its left.

The approach to Bethecar Moor, With Arnsbarrow Hill on the skyline

The next two miles are recommended only in clear weather. If the clouds are low enough to obscure the tops, then it would be wiser to remain on the main path across the moor. After a good mile, this joins a broad green trackway (the drive to Parkamoor) to which the main route will descend from Top o'Selside.

Leaving the path, keep right of the marsh, using vague sheeptrods to reach the foot of the hill. On this steep section a path can be found on which to make the pleasant climb to the heathery top, passing, en route, above the only craggy outcrop of the day. A neat summit cairn is in place, with a little edge on which to sit and absorb the scene, makes this a super place to be, amongst the bilberry and heather. At the approximate height of 1040ft, this cairn does not quite mark the highest point, which is another twenty or so feet higher on the next rise to the north. The 'adopted' top does, however, fit the bill better, with its shapelier look and tremendously extensive views. A smallish portion of Coniston Water sits in front of Torver, with Dow Crag rearing up behind, and the remaining Coniston Fells outspread to its right. Ahead also is a packed line-up of central and eastern fells, far beyond the rolling landscape of Grizedale Forest.

On leaving, head north again on a path which soon peters out in a depression. A faint trod to the right picks up the way, but this too fades, to leave us striking out for the final yards onto the broader main top. This is colourful country, full of interest with a well built stone fold abutting onto the rocks, the nearby largest of which proves to mark the summit of the fell. *Continue onward through the sea of heather, and over a minor knoll the circular Arnsbarrow Tarn appears ahead. Drop down to it, skirting the marshy area of the outflow by keeping to the higher ground to the right.*

Arnsbarrow Hill and Tarn from Top o'Selside

From above Arnsbarrow Tarn a useful trod works round to the gently rising slopes that culminate in the cairn on Top o'Selside. The outstanding panorama is dominated, perhaps inevitably, by the Coniston Fells, though there are also all the features of the previous hill's view of course. Coniston village makes a welcome appearance several miles in advance, its setting beneath its fells seen to full advantage. Curiously the lake itself seems to have disappeared, but by standing plum on the cairn, a tiny section of its foot, at Nibthwaite, is revealed: fear not - this situation will soon be remedied, and how!

Top o' Selside
1099' △ • • •

Grizedale
Forest

Arnsbarrow ⊘ 45
Tarn

1056' ✕

Arnsbarrow
Hill

1037' △

Stang
Moss →

Bethecar
Moor

44

Summit cairn,
Arnsbarrow Hill

On the true summit
of Arnsbarrow Hill:

left - the sheepfold

below - summit rocks

Leave Top o'Selside in a south-westerly direction, a thin but clear path descending through bracken, fairly steeply, for 300ft. It splits midway, that contouring initially to the right proving to land plum on the junction where the moor-traverse path joins the Parkamoor drive. The left branch meets the path a little earlier, which is no great hardship. Turn right along the delectable green trackway as it contours the fellside, and savour fully the views over the lake, now revealed almost in its entirety. *At a fork with the abandoned farm of Low Parkamoor on the rising slope ahead, turn down to it, the track descends to cross a stream before rising to the house.*

Pass along the front to find a green path curving left up the field behind. A fence comes in and shadows it along to a gate. From the stile here the unkempt terrain of The Park is entered. The objective is the forest ahead, where it will be entered over to the left, behind the knolls of Park Crags. Two entirely different paths set forth for this. The first attempts to trace the bridleway, heads straight off, sketchily crossing the moister central section before bearing left to climb the last of the knolls: it joins the forest fence too far right, necessitating a slight descent left to locate the gate and stile.

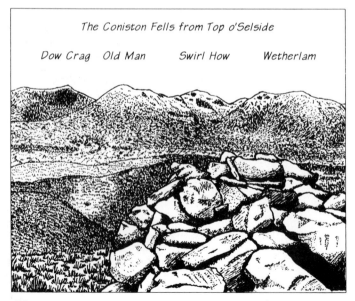

The Coniston Fells from Top o'Selside

Dow Crag   Old Man   Swirl How   Wetherlam

The left-hand path sees more use, certainly from mountain bikes, and though drier and clearer, its more appealing line over the lumps and bumps does not follow the right of way. Just before reaching the forest, unparalleled views of the lake can be enjoyed from the edge of the steep drop, with the entire upper reach revealed far below, a veritable bird's-eye view. **The forest path is easy to follow as it heads off** *through a felled landscape that is stranger than the forestry itself. For some time then, we can can enjoy extended views over the lake to the fells.* **A forest road is met before long, and can be follow along to the left at a spanking pace.** *Ahead, the Fairfield horseshoe is well displayed, with Dollywaggon Pike's slopes rising to mighty Helvellyn. Over to the left are the fells around Langdale, with Harrison Stickle and Pavey Ark on show.*

Grizedale
Forest

Park
Crags

The
Park

Low
Parkamoor   ×High
              Parkamoor

Top
o'Selside

The area known as Grizedale Forest is a vast tract of high country between Hawkshead and Coniston Water. Though heavily planted between the wars, and now the Forestry Commission's pride and joy, its history goes much deeper. The land was owned by the monks of Furness Abbey, who as early as the 13th century put much woodland to the axe to provide more grazing land. The present owners are now drawing large numbers of visitors by way of a wildlife centre, woodland walks, and a variety of other attractions.

Coniston Water is the fourth largest of the English lakes, and until 1974 it was the major lake of Lancashire. Five miles in length, its typical pencil shape is a legacy of the Ice age. A string of famous names have had strong connections with the lake. Three, in chronological order, are John Ruskin, Arthur Ransome and Donald Campbell. Ruskin, outstanding Victorian artist, poet, critic and early environmentalist, spent the last 30 years of his life at Brantwood, overlooking the lake, and the village has long boasted a Ruskin Museum.

Ransome the author was best known for his popular children's adventure "Swallows and Amazons", set on and around two islands near the foot of the lake. Campbell was the brave world water speed record breaker so tragically killed while attempting to beat his own record here in January 1967. The Sun Hotel in the village, where he stayed, contains mementoes of his time here.

A most pleasing sight on the lake is the Victorian steam yacht Gondola. After almost 80 years service it ceased operating in 1937, but after 40 dormant years the National Trust painstakingly restored it to its former glory, and this elegant craft resumed its former role in 1980. It plys the lake daily from April to October, and breaks journey at Park-a-Moor, on the south-eastern shore beneath Top o'Selside, and also at Brantwood. A cultured conclusion to the day would be a visit to Brantwood and entry into Coniston by steam yacht!

The steam yacht Gondola on Coniston Water

GRIZEDALE FOREST TO CONISTON WATER

Remain on the forest road until a gentle rise is reached. At the top, look for a grassy gap in the trees, which doubles back to the left carrying a good, clear path. This drops down to cross another forest road in a large clearing in the vicinity of the old farmhouse at Lawson Park. Its origins date back to medieval times, when it was - like Parkamoor before it - a sheep farm under the auspices of Furness Abbey. **Now signed towards Coniston, the bridleway bends down to the right, and free of regimented plantations it descends at a gentle gradient past much more natural woodland interspersed with bracken.**

One tempting diversion is a link path on the Brantwood nature trail. This development provides an opportunity to visit the lovely house of Brantwood. This was the home of John Ruskin from 1872 up to his death in 1900 (see further note in Coniston Water section, opposite). Within is a large collection of Ruskin's drawings and watercolours. Other attractions are a crafts and picture gallery, a bookshop, a 'Wainwright Gallery', tearoom, and special themed events.

The track runs gently down to the road along the eastern shore of Coniston Water. Turn right and it leads, quite literally, to Waterhead. Here is Monk Coniston car park and toilets.

Waterhead

Coniston Water

50

49

Brantwood

Crag
Head

Lawson
Park

49

Grizedale Forest

Coniston is the most colourful village encountered on the Furness Way, though Cartmel might argue. It is one of the Lake District's premier centres, and a consequence of this is vast crowds of summer visitors thronging the streets and the lakeshore. A further result is a heavy strain on accommodation resources, though two youth hostels and a campsite make life easier. As with all the district's larger villages, casual visitors far outweigh serious walkers.

The attractive slate buildings shelter beneath towering fells, crowned by the Old Man of Coniston himself, from whose very slopes much of the slate was won. Though Coniston's chief industry may be tourism, a number of local people still find employment in quarrying.

The most interesting building is Coniston Hall, a late 16th century manor house tucked away from the village near the lakeshore. Its great round chimneys feature prominently. More centrally placed is St. Andrew's church, dating from 1819, built of local slate and with a most spacious interior.

In the churchyard is a large Anglo-saxon-type cross commemorating John Ruskin, who died here in 1900 - Coniston churchyard was his preference to Westminster Abbey. A museum was opened in the village centre shortly after his death, while Brantwood, already passed across the lake, is of course open to visitors. Also of local slate is the Campbell memorial, which takes the form of a T-shaped seat arrangement on the little green. Do not be misled by memorials, however, for the village of Coniston is very much alive, with a healthy air about its busy streets.

Ruskin Cross,
St Andrew's
church,
Coniston

From the head of the lake either remain on the road to the Hawkshead junction then go left on the parallel path, or for a break from routine one can join the trippers on the shore, following it round to the right as far as possible before being deflected up onto the road on reaching private ground. Here the parallel enclosed path can be picked up to head for the village,

Yewdale Beck being crossed en route.

The Black Bull, Coniston

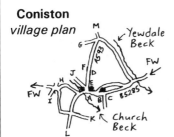

Coniston
village plan

A - St Andrew's church
B - bus stops/toilets
C - Campbell memorial
D - Information Centre
E - Post office
F - Ruskin Museum
G - to Coniston Far End youth hostel
H - Sun Hotel
I - old railway station
J - to Coppermines youth hostel
K - to boat landings
L - to Broughton
M - to Ambleside

SECTION 5

——— CONISTON TO BOOT ———

13 miles   3000 feet of ascent

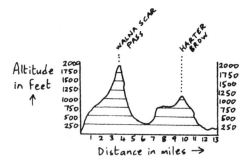

This penultimate day requires the most effort, although gradients are, on the whole, fairly gentle. The centuries old Walna Scar track climbs to almost 2000ft as it leads over the Coniston Fells to Seathwaite in the Duddon Valley - ideally placed for well earned mid-walk refreshment. The second half of the day entails a crossing of the shoulder of Harter Fell, to descend amidst glorious views into Eskdale.

At the old corn mill, Boot

CONISTON TO BOO TARN

To leave the village, start from the church gate and cross the road bridge over Church Beck in the village centre. Turn right immediately, up a lane between a cafe and the beck, to pass the Sun Hotel. The lane meets another road on a bend, with the former station just over to the left. Passing an old signpost to 'Old Man, Walna Scar and Seathwaite', *the road at once begins an ultra-steep climb alongside a small beck. This is the start of the Walna Scar Road, and as the gradients soon ease one can settle down to a relaxing stroll up to the fell gate,* enjoying a fine prospect of the ravaged Coniston mountains.

The Walna Scar Road - sensibly re-classified as a bridleway - was once an important route across the hills.
The laden ponies that once came this way have long been replaced by laden walkers, none more so than those on the Furness Way!

At the gate onto the fell the dismaying sight of car-borne walkers gearing up should be ignored, and sights set on the broad track bearing off to the left. Near-level walking leads quickly to the reedy pool that is Boo Tarn. Leaving the track here is a remarkably graded quarry track, up which I have watched with alarm great waggons negotiate the zigzags. Slate won from high on the slopes of the Old Man has lost out over the years to cheap foreign imports. Here also, a smashing green path commences an unfrequented climb to the summit of the Old Man.

At Boo Tarn

71

*Cove Bridge,
looking to
Buck Pike and
Dow Crag*

The compact group of mountains known as the Coniston Fells rise between the upper Duddon Valley and Coniston itself, a clutch of distinct summits rising above the 2500ft line. Easy connecting ridges make a complete traverse quite reasonable within a single fellwalk, and for this reason a second overnight in Coniston may be deemed worthwhile, to also enjoy the luxury of a light pack! By turning their backs on the Duddon, these fells show their true allegiance by displaying their finest features to Coniston.

The most impressive single feature, however, is the mighty rockface of Dow Crag, hidden from Coniston by the Old Man. Coniston Old Man is the summit of the group, and by far the most popular, though Swirl How, further north and only inches lower, has far and away the important pivotal role.

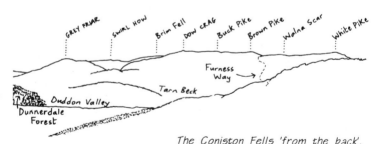

*The Coniston Fells 'from the back'.
Our route of descent to the Duddon Valley is here seen from later
in the day, near Stonythwaite, four miles ahead*

72

The track continues unerringly: faulty navigation here should leave serious question marks about a future in rambling. Remarkably, I have watched folk drive their little hatchbacks as far along this bridleway as possible before disembarking to pull on their gear. How close do they want to get, and how on earth would they manage in Scotland, where the mountains aren't already on the doorstep of the B + B?

After a lengthy level section the track finally begins to climb in earnest. It passes between two rock gateways to reach a conspicuous cairn. *This signals the departure of a popular path to Goat's Water, and the ridge between the Old Man and Dow Crag. For rock climbers, it is the yellow brick road to the magnificent playground of the latter.* *The main path continues, soon rising to the fine stone arch of Cove Bridge.* *This old packhorse bridge blends effortlessly into its surrounds, and the tumbling beck suggest a refreshment halt.*

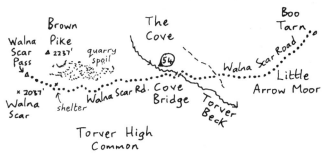

Rising away from the beck across the moor, the path soon steepens as it encounters a more typical Lakeland terrain. Well-made zigzags lead the way up through rougher ground, which melts away again as the gradients ease to approach the summit of the pass. A small cairn marks the spot, in a setting that is again more moor-like in nature.

Fellow walkers may well now head up to the right, where the gradients return for a lengthy climb to Dow Crag. To the left, easier slopes quickly cease on the gentle 'top' of Walna Scar itself, just breaking the 2000ft mark.

Holy Trinity, Seathwaite

Though little more than a hamlet, Seathwaite is a welcoming little place, the highest in the dale. In this peaceful setting, with the beck nearby and the fells rising grandly above, there is a strong temptation to linger on a hot summer's day. The little church was built in 1874, and is the last resting place of the Rev. Robert Walker. Known as Wonderful Walker, he was 60 years vicar of Seathwaite, and it is recorded he left a remarkable £2000 from an annual stipend that never exceeded £50. A Postbus service provides a link with Broughton in Furness.

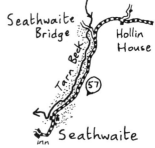

Harter Fell and the Scafells from Long House Gill

WALNA SCAR TO SEATHWAITE

Descent to the Duddon Valley is rapid, and full of interest. The path is excellent and so are the views, with shapely Harter Fell looking especially attractive, a real pyramid of a mountain. **Initially well graded to permit large strides, the track swings right before the old Walna Scar Quarries to begin a more determined descent. Long House Gill comes in for company as the track meets up with a water authority road coming down from Seathwaite Tarn. This takes over the running to drop past Long House Farm, to then quickly join the narrow road that threads its way up the** *valley. Just below is the arched Seathwaite Bridge on Tarn Beck.*

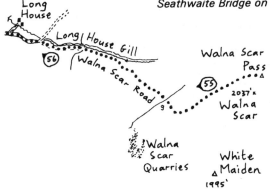

One of the quirks of the Duddon Valley is the presence of Tarn Beck, which runs a parallel course to the river for some distance, and thereby confuses many visitors into thinking they're enjoying the Duddon's company! **Turn left on the valley road for a gentle half-mile amble into Seathwaite.** *On this long day over the hills, the attractions of the* Newfield Inn, *the sole source of refreshment, will be spurned by few!*

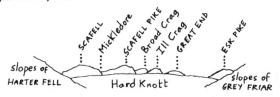

The Scafells from Long House Gill - as illustrated opposite

75

Suitably refreshed, continue down the lane for less than 200 yards, then take a gate where a permitted path (to avoid dodgy stepping stones) heads off into the trees. A concrete footbridge spans Tarn Beck, and the path heads away into more trees. Rising over a brow it descends to meet a path alongside the Duddon. Follow the main river upstream to reach very servicable stepping stones in beautiful woodland surrounds. Should this challenge prove a little daunting, the unenthusiastic can opt for the graceful footbridge just upstream.

The river Duddon is a real pearl, immortalised by Wordsworth who penned nearly three dozen sonnets in its praise. Marking the old Cumberland-Furness (Lancashire) boundary throughout its length, the river is born on the fells above the Wrynose Pass. It quickly forms a valley that remains narrow and fell-bound almost all the way to the Irish Sea, where a major estuary is formed. The Duddon Sands are an immeasurably valuable habitat for wading birds, yet there are those would see a barrage built to stem the tides and make life a little easier for road traffic.

Also sad, but not nearly so catastrophic, is the fact that **our route now foregoes the Duddon's company by heading directly away, also leaving the woods by means of a gate. The farm of High Wallowbarrow stands just ahead, and is reached by a path through a couple of fields.** Wallowbarrow Crag is seen at its finest from this point, as it towers menacingly above.

Leave the yard by a gate just to the right of the house, and follow a track straight up the hill to another gate. From it the path climbs through bracken to a gate admitting to the woods. A good zigzag eases the steep going, and on crossing Rake Beck emerges into open air again. When opportunity arises, look back across the valley to see the shapely cone of Caw - a smaller version of Harter Fell - and the even more diminutive Stickle Pike, which tapers into a fine peak.

*Wallowbarrow Crag
from Seathwaite*

Below:
High Wallowbarrow

Below:
Footbridge over
the Duddon,
near Seathwaite

Now well above Rake Beck, the path rises across the fell under the forbidding crag to eventually level out amid outcrops of heather. A track to the hidden Stonythwaite is joined, and followed to the right between small rock outcrops and tangles of heather. On rounding a corner an outstanding view opens out: across the upper Duddon are the Coniston Fells, (our descent from Walna Scar featuring prominently) while ahead are the higher mountains in the heart of Lakeland, dominated for now by the graceful pyramid of Bowfell. Harter Fell, whose slopes we're on, is impressive right above us. This undulating green trackway leads unerringly to Grassguards.

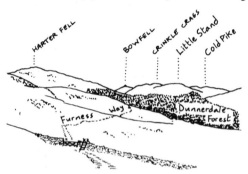

The view north from above Stonythwaite

Pass through the farmyard at this isolated spot, and immediately after the last building, go up to a gate on the left. Ignoring first a concrete ford and then a footbridge, a delightful but short section ensues as the lively Grassguards Gill leads up to a stile by a gate. Beyond is the terminus of a forest road coming in from the mature Dunnerdale Forest, while to the left are younger plantings. Advance straight up, a little marshily, and take a simple footbridge over the stream on the right (or cross almost at once to gain a slender tongue between tinkling streams). A drier path heads up past the basic footbridge. Like Grizedale before it, the devastation of felled areas looks far worse than the dreary plantations ever did!

The path remains thin but clear. Grassguards Gill offers pleasant company for the most part, though we are deflected away by a side-stream for a short while before returning to it. With a wall in view ahead, another fork of streams is reached - a bridleway sign for Eskdale sends us right to cross the gill to a gate in the forest fence. Here we enter the felled area, not a pretty sight though all concentration will be on tracing a slender, partly obscured path.

It bears up to the left, soon reaching a better defined path when a forest road comes in from the right to end here. Go left along this, rising just a touch and then forging on towards the brow. The first

WALLOWBARROW TO SPOTHOW GILL

When the Forestry Commission takes great pride in multi-coloured trails around some of their plantations, you would think they might make a better job of identifying a long-established bridleway linking two of the very finest valleys in the National Park!

continued
long-awaited view into Eskdale is, in keeping with, the last stage of the climb, something of a let-down: ahead, the first sighting is merely the back of Illgill Head and Whin Rigg, which display on their other side the remarkable Wastwater Screes.

The trees end at the brow of the hill. Here gratefully take a gate out of the plantation and pause to relax. We're on the very top of Harter Brow now, with Green Crag over to the left beyond an uninviting moss, and a thin path climbing right to scale Harter Fell: the very fit might consider a detour to climb this mountain, which rises a further thousand feet. **Ignoring a stile in the fence down to the left, resume in the same direction on a much improved path through the broad, undulating pass,** amidst heather and bracken and with constantly improving views over Eskdale.

First the Pillar group appears, then **on reaching a third stile in the fence at a point where it parts company with the beck, this is the point we leave the clear path. Above is a perched boulder,** while yards further along the path is a prize moment as the entire cirque of fells hemming in upper Eskdale appear. The finest mountain scene in England is on display, from Scafell to Crinkle Crags.

79

Back at the stile, cross both fence and beck (shadowed by a collapsed wall on the near side) to follow a slender green path through the bracken. Within two minutes we are greeted by a classic Eskdale prospect, this time the inviting green floor: in view are the houses of Boot and a scattering of whitewashed farms. This completes the full panorama, mountains and valley: Harter Fell too has taken greater shape now.

Passing beneath a rocky knoll, the thin path descends then runs level again, even to the point of re-ascending a few feet and instilling a little doubt as to its purpose. Forge on a little, however, and a series of small cairns offer assistance as the way turns down to the right to make a more concerted and clearer descent to the intake wall that appears below. After crossing the foot of a deep-set gill (a grand spot) turn left with the wall, on a clearer path to shortly descend to a gate. Drop down through the field (over to the right see the zigzagging tortures of the Hardknott Pass) *below to join a tractor-track, this being followed left to the attractive farmstead of Penny Hill.* Friendly and enthusiastic dogs greet you.

Pass along the front of the farmhouse and out along the drive to reach the small but attractive Doctor Bridge. This is a stone structure not a medical person, though to be fair it was built by a doctor who lived at Penny Hill. Downstream, but high on the skyline is Birker Force tumbling over the fellside. Cross the Esk here, a brief acquaintance that will be strengthened tomorrow. Pause on the bridge to peer into the sparkling clarity of the Esk. If not heading for the hostel or Boot, then turn left over the bridge to follow a truly exquisite path downstream to St Catherine's church, a beautiful walk, and one that can be done even if you are heading for Boot, if so desired. The way needs little explaining: part-way along the path leaves the river for a spell, delightfully enclosed by walls at times, in a quiet backwater that could be anywhere.

Over the bridge, turn right along the lane which rises to meet the narrow road winding through the floor of Eskdale. If the youth hostel is your objective, then turn right for a ten minute walk past the Woolpack Inn.

Penny Hill

Doctor Bridge

*The mountains of upper Eskdale
from the slopes of Harter Fell*

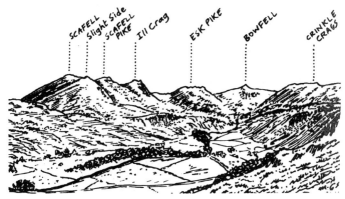

The tiny community of Boot is the first of any size in Eskdale. It stand just off the valley road on a cul-de-sac lane. Around a century ago iron ore was won from the fellsides above, and taken down the valley on the railway (which at that time was not the narrow gauge we see today). Boot's two most interesting features stand together at the head of the village. The present packhorse bridge is over 250 years old, and from it a popular walkers' path now leads over Burnmoor Tarn to Wasdale Head. At one time it served as a corpse road for Wasdale's dead to be buried over here.

Beside the bridge is the old corn mill, one of at least three that operated on Whillan Beck. Dating from 1578, cereal was ground here until well into the 20th century. Admirably restored by the county council in 1975, with its two working waterwheels it is open to the public from Easter to September (closed Mondays). Included is an exhibition of the mill's historic past.

The packhorse bridge
and corn mill, Boot

To get to Boot, go left for a short quarter-mile along the road, then turn right along a drive to Christcliff, signed to Stony Tarn and Eel Tarn. Just before the buildings, take a gate on the left signed to Boot. Cross the top side of the field to a gap-stile opposite, then pass through a gate at the far right corner to enter the farmyard of Paddock Wray. Follow the drive out at the other side, and when it turns sharp left for the road, go straight ahead, over a stile to find a cracking stile built into the wall. Through the tiniest possible triangular wooded enclosure and out by another hoary old stile. On emerging, we can see AND hear Birker Force on the skyline opposite: note also the remarkable girth of some of these walls. Head along the field bottoms with a wall on the left, to arrive through a strip of undergrowth at Hollins Farm (camping).

Don't follow the drive out, but seek out a gate on the right at the end of a short-lived way after the last building. Again along a field bottom, through a kissing-gate with Boot appearing just in front. Beyond a stile cross a field top beneath trees to reach a slender gap-stile which empties onto a steep lane. Turn left to descend by the boisterous Whillan Beck into Boot. Across the beck are the waterwheels of the corn mill.

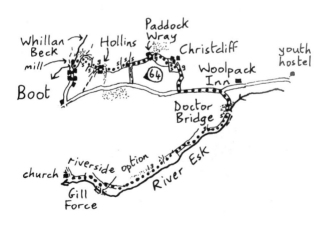

83

SECTION 6

——— BOOT TO RAVENGLASS ———

10½ miles   1050 feet of ascent

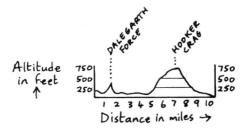

Altitude
in feet
↑

DALEGARTH FORCE   HOOKER CRAG

750 750
500 500
250 250

1 2 3 4 5 6 7 8 9 10
Distance in miles →

The final day provides a chance to wind down, with an easy but very scenic 10½ miles down to the sea. Again it's a walk of two halves, the first being in the valley of the lovely Esk (including a visit to a splendid waterfall), the second being high above it on a full length traverse of Muncaster Fell. The splendour of Muncaster Castle and the Roman ruins of Walls Castle ensure interest is maintained to the very end, to the final yards along the beach into Ravenglass.

Boot

BOOT TO ST CATHERINE'S CHURCH

Leave Boot by the lane down to the valley road. Just two minutes along to the right is the terminus, at Dalegarth station, of the *Ravenglass & Eskdale Railway.* **Cross straight over and down a lane to reach the isolated church** in an idyllic setting by the river Esk. Within its yard note the carved stone of Tommy Dobson, a celebrated master of the local pack of foxhounds (illustrated overleaf). The grassy riverbank sward is a grand place to linger, perhaps on the memorial seat to Roland Taylor, 1907-1992, a founder and lifelong stalwart of Whitehaven Rambling Club.

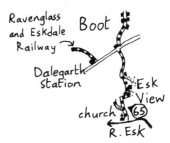

St Catherine's church

The Esk rises as a mountain stream in the heart of England's highest fells, the Scafell group. It descends from around 2400 feet to only 400 feet in a mere 5 miles, and remains incredibly clear and sparkling throughout its journey. Our acquaintance with it coincides with its more sedate passage between richly wooded banks and green pastures. Within the bounds of the valley, the Esk gives its name to village, railway and a near-3000ft peak.

If the river is sufficiently low, stepping stones can be used to gain the opposite bank, turning downstream on a good path through bracken to enter woodland. A footbridge over Stanley Gill is followed by a field crossing to reach the main route on a track climbing from Dalegarth Hall.

Assuming the stepping stones look unappealing, return just a short way along the lane and turn left along a super green bridleway, winding between walls and then into a leafier passage to emerge above the river on the drive to Dalegarth Hall. Turn left, crossing Trough House Bridge, a lovely wooded dell where the river flows through a rocky gorge. A car park just beyond is the source of the holidaymakers around here. **Just beyond is a fork. The hall drive goes right, our way goes left, quickly rising to meet the 'stepping stones' route at a crossroads of pathways.**

It is from here the detour to Dalegarth Force can be made. It demands only a half-hour, and is worth every minute of it. Turn up the track, and leave very soon by a gate on the left to re-enter the wooded environs of Stanley Gill. A delightful path leads up alongside the beck. As the ravine narrows, the beck is crossed three times by footbridges. The last of these is the viewpoint for the falls, and the terminus of the path. Savour the scene, then return to the path above Dalegarth Hall.

Dalegarth Hall is an interesting old farmstead, formerly a large manor house. It is perhaps most notable for its large, rounded chimneys.

Dalegarth Hall

Tommy Dobson's memorial,
St Catherine's church

Dalegarth Force

Resume where we left off, heading behind Dalegarth Hall where a stile and sign point the way to Forge Bridge. Across a field we plunge into the rich woodland of Low Wood on a pleasant cart track. The way remains clear as it emerges to hear the welcome sound of the river: just below is a rocky bank that begs a look. A path runs on through an area of riverside scrub, then the way cuts a bend of the Esk before rejoining it for the last stage to Forge Bridge, by way of a farm drive. Turn right to cross the river, noting first its unchanged clarity since we met it at Doctor Bridge, and then at last a prospect of our final obstacle, the hitherto secretive Muncaster Fell directly downstream. For now, however, simply *turn along the lane for two minutes to the prominent* George IV *inn.*

After partaking of any suitable refreshment, continue up the road towards Eskdale Green. Here we are on the fringe of this scattered village, whose railway station is our point of departure from the road.

The Ravenglass & Eskdale Railway was opened in 1875 to transport iron ore from the Eskdale mines to the main line at Ravenglass. In no time at all it was also carrying passengers. From the demise of that particular venture to its acquisition by a preservation society in the early 1960s, it had a chequered history. It was opened and closed numerous times, and almost disappeared completely. Today it is a highly successful operation, and every year thousands travel its colourful course, on what is now a narrow-gauge line - known as La'al (Little) Ratty. At least one of several steam engines is usually in action, and certainly it makes a temptingly quick way of reaching the end of the Furness Way!

The River Mite

Muncaster Fell
from the Esk
at Forge Bridge

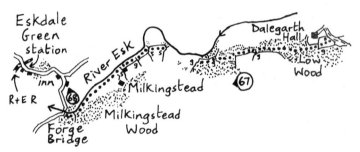

King George IV
Eskdale Green

Just before the road bridges the railway at the Green, leave by an enclosed cart track to the left. As this rises to cross the railway by Eskdale Green station, don't cross but bear left along an inviting enclosed pathway. A tiny stream crossing leads into the bottom corner of an enclosure rife with over-enthusiastic bushes. Remain with a wall on the left to evade their clutches, and when free of them, bear right across the open field to join a wall enclosing a wood. Follow it past a wooded knoll on the left, then head directly across the field to locate a gate in the wall beneath the rising slopes of Muncaster Fell. Pass through and go right a few feet along the track, then turn up to the left on a clear path that rises through rampant scrub to reach a kissing-gate onto the fell proper.

Already we can enjoy a fine panorama back up Eskdale, with the houses of Eskdale Green and many other valley features beneath Scafell, Bowfell, Crinkle Crags and Harter Fell, a magnificent mountain line-up.

A clear and excellent (made) path scales the bracken-clad fellside, soon easing out on a shoulder just beneath the minor, heathery top of Silver Knott. Ahead the length of Muncaster Fell is now revealed, with its summit Hooker Crag in sight, and a goodly expanse of sea with the Esk undergoing its final section down to the left.

After a slight dip the path climbs near a wall, and passing through a gateway it bears left to cross a slightly marshy tract decorated with a sea of cotton-grass. Just around the corner the path reaches a small table-like group of stones. This is Ross's Camp, because its says it is, and also bears the year 1883. It was apparently the handiwork of a Victorian shooting party, and stills serves its role as a 'dining table' well today, a splendid perch from which to survey journey's end. Also view the great length of the unsung Black Combe ridge southwards beyond the lower Esk valley.

Muncaster Fell

Ross's
Camp

758

Hooker
Crag

The path continues, retaining its excellent views of lower Eskdale, but with Hooker Crag re-appearing now only a short stroll away. Another marsh (rampant cotton grass) is skirted before the path forks. Take the right one to climb steeply and rapidly to the OS column (S5768) on Hooker Crag. This rugged little upthrust of rocks serve to confirm Hooker Crag's superiority over the rest of Muncaster Fell. This truly stunning viewpoint has just about everything: a wide spread of the coast contrasting sharply with the great build-up of mountains around the head of Eskdale. Turn the page and make the most of this one, as I did!

Hooker Crag,
looking to Scafell

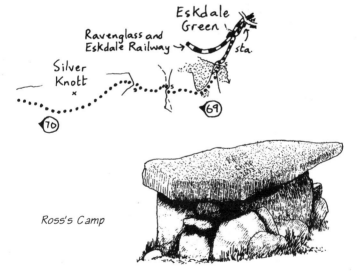

Eskdale
Green

Ravenglass and
Eskdale Railway →

sta.

Silver
Knott
×

69

70

Ross's Camp

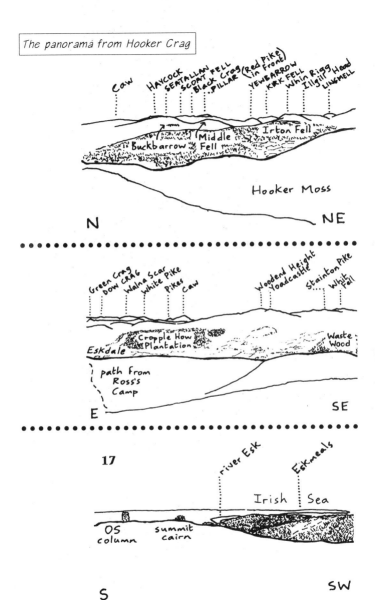

The panorama from Hooker Crag

Caw · HAYCOCK · SEATALLAN · SCOAT FELL · Black Crag · PILLAR (Red Pike) in front · YEWBARROW · KIRK FELL · Whin Rigg · Illgill Head · LINGMELL

Buckbarrow · Middle Fell · Irton Fell

Hooker Moss

N   NE

Green Crag · Dow CRAG · Walna Scar · White Pike · Pikes · Caw · Woodend Height · Yoadcastle · Stainton Pike · Whit Fell

Eskdale · Cropple How Plantation · Waste Wood

path from Ross's Camp

E   SE

river Esk · Eskmeals

Irish Sea

OS column · summit cairn

S   SW

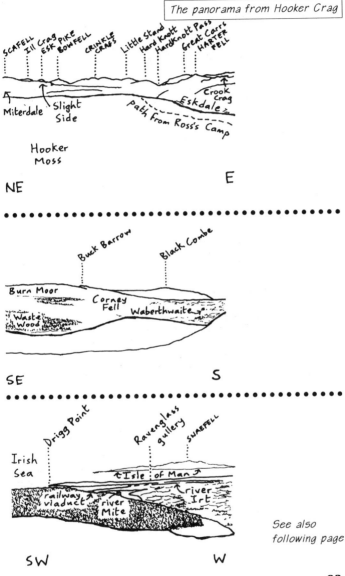

The panorama from Hooker Crag

SCAFELL · Ill Crag · ESK PIKE · BOWFELL · CRINKLE CRAGS · Little Stand · Hard Knott · Hardknott Pass · Great Carrs · HARTER FELL

Crook Crag
Eskdale
Miterdale · Slight Side
Path from Ross's Camp

Hooker Moss

NE   E

Buck Barrow   Black Combe
Burn Moor   Corney Fell
Waste Wood   Waberthwaite

SE   S

Drigg Point   Ravenglass gullery · SWAEFELL
Irish Sea
Isle of Man
railway viaduct · river Mite · river Irt

See also following page

SW   W

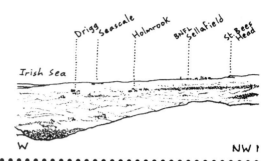

Drigg Seascale Holmrook BNFL Sellafield St Bees Head

Irish Sea

W   NW ↑

Vacate Hooker Crag on the path which appears to be making a bee-line for Ravenglass. It drops to a wood corner and continues on a broader track to shortly become an enclosed woodland cart track. Already the influence of Muncaster Castle is strong, in the park-like surround of rhododendron bushes and a fine variety of trees. *This delectable, leafy byway slowly descends the long sprawling ridge of the fell, becoming a more solid track before debouching onto a sharp bend of the A595 coast road.*

A left turn along the road (with footway) leads to a drive into the otherwise firmly enclosed grounds of Muncaster Castle. Head straight down it, first item of interest being St Michael's church, embowered in trees in a quiet corner. *The drive descends past a nursery to the heart of the grounds. To the right is the owl centre, to the left the castle. Cross straight over the trackway here,* confirmed by waymarks, across a lawn and past a duckpond to join another track. This is followed left for only yards before heading up a narrower path which forks right through the trees of Dovecot Wood.

Leaving Hooker Crag for Ravenglass

94

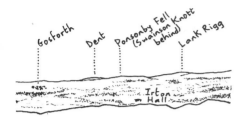

NW .... N

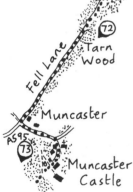

Hooker Crag

If desperate to reach Ravenglass, then on joining the A595, head straight down it. This is an uninspiring finish that should be invoked only as a last resort.

Lych-gate,
Muncaster church

Muncaster Castle is an enormous sandstone structure enclosed by beautiful grounds renowned for their rhododendron display. The house began life, like so many before it this week, as a 14th century pele tower, and the building we see today is largely little more than a century old.

It has been in the possession of the Lords of Muncaster, the Pennington family, since the days of the pele tower, and these days is shared for a few hours daily with the paying public. Inside are beautiful portraits and furniture.

Outside, too, is a great deal of interest, in particular the owl centre, which plays an important role in the conservation and breeding of a wide range of owls. Many of these are on view, and most afternoons will see some of them released for flying within the grounds.

The gardens and owl centre are open throughout the year, while the house is open from mid-March to October (but not on Mondays).

Muncaster Castle, west front

MUNCASTER CASTLE TO WALLS CASTLE

On entering Dovecot Wood, a most enjoyable woodland climb ensues. Early gaps in the trees afford a brief glimpse back to the castle. *As the climbing ceases and the trees thin out a little, bear right on the main path to reach the edge of the wood. A kissing-gate and stile in the substantial park wall see us scratching our heads over the sudden disappearance of such an excellent path. Fear not: head south-west across this vast expanse of open parkland, aiming to the left of the woods that successfully keep Ravenglass hidden from view.*

Now we have the finest views of the arrangement of the estuary, with sand dune arms protecting the natural harbour. *On nearing a fenced plantation, keep eyes peeled for a step-stile. A clear path descends through this small, new plantation, emerging via a gate alongside the farm buildings at Newtown.* A sign on the gate informs us that this has been a permissive path - the true right of way must be buried somewhere in the plantations.

Bear right along the drive, which leads pleasantly along to a junction in front of the impressive looking Walls Mansion. A right turn here leads to the ruins of Walls Castle.

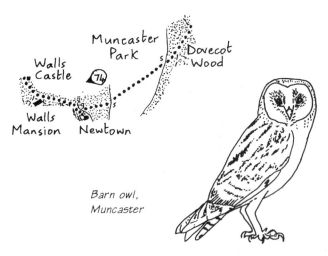

Barn owl,
Muncaster

Ravenglass is the end of the road, and as if to emphasise this point its main street runs as far as possible before literally dropping onto the beach. Although fairly and squarely on the coast, Ravenglass is sheltered from the worst excesses of the weather due to the indentations of the coastline hereabouts: although only as dunes, land reaches out another mile further west in the form of the two outer arms of the estuaries of the rivers Irt and Esk. Immediately in front of Ravenglass they join forces with the smaller river Mite, and together head out to sea as the Esk. Nowhere else on the Cumbrian coast is quite like this, and the extensive dunes are designated a nature reserve, including Britain's largest colony of black headed gulls. There is history here too, for Ravenglass boasted one of Cumberland's first markets, as far back as 1308.

The village consists of little more than its main street and the environs of the railway - the Ravenglass & Eskdale Railway has its headquarters here, where there is a museum, gift shop, information office and cafe. There is a good 'railway pub' in the old station itself, while refreshments can also be found on the main street, which also plays host to a more traditional hotel bearing the arms of the family from the 'big house'. Were it not for the railway, then Ravenglass really would be a quiet place. Ravenglass itself has not cashed in on the visitors brought down by the little trains, indeed next to this, Arnside almost resembles Blackpool. A chap on Hooker Crag warned me before my first visit that it was the most inhospitable place he had ever been, and in a howling gale, with the pubs shut, he could have a point... In truth though, its simple peacefulness is an attraction in itself - a relaxing location to finish the walk. And don't forget, there's still a grown-up train to whisk you back to the outside world.

Main Street,
Ravenglass

After an inspection of Walls Castle, resume along the drive a short distance (the unexcavated fort platform is on our left) **to locate a branch path going under the railway and onto the beach.** A few fishing boats still bob about. **Ravenglass is at last visible, and within two minutes is reached.**

If a high tide rules the beach out of bounds, return to the drive to reach a road: here a footpath goes left over a railway bridge, passing both the railway stations to reach the front.

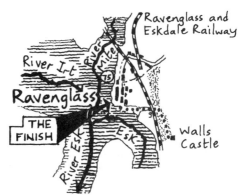

Many centuries ago Ravenglass was a port of much importance, and used as such by the Romans. they built a fort - Glannoventa - on which now stands Walls Mansion. Of most interest now are the remains of Walls Castle, thought to have been a bathhouse. The walls are said to be the tallest surviving non-military Roman remains in the country.

Walls Castle,
Ravenglass

RECORD OF THE JOURNEY

Date	Place	Miles		Times		Comments
		daily	total	arrive	depart	
	Arnside	–	–			
	Hazelslack	1 ¾	1 ¾			
	Haverbrack	3 ½	3 ½			
	Milnthorpe	4 ½	4 ½			
	Heversham	5 ¾	5 ¾			
	Sizergh Castle	9 ½	9 ½			
	Helsington Church	10 ¾	10 ¾			
	Brigsteer	11 ¼	11 ¼			
	Crosthwaite	15	15			
	Lord's Seat, Whitbarrow	3 ½	18 ½			
	Witherslack Hall	4 ½	19 ½			
	Witherslack Church	6	21			
	River Winster	7 ¾	22 ¾			
	Lindale	9 ¾	24 ¾			
	Hampsfell	11 ½	26 ½			
	Cartmel	13	28			
	Bigland Tarn	4 ¾	32 ¾			
	Low Wood	5 ¾	33 ¾			
	Greenodd	8	36			

Date	Place	Miles		Times		Comments
		daily	total	arrive	depart	
	Spark Bridge	10 ½	38 ½			
	Lowick Green	11 ¼	39 ¼			
	Lowick Bridge	12 ½	40 ½			
	Stock	2	42 ½			
	Arnsbarrow Hill	4	44 ½			
	Top o'Selside	5	45 ½			
	Grizedale Forest	6 ½	47			
	Lawson Park	8	48 ½			
	Waterhead	10	50 ½			
	Coniston	11	51 ½			
	Boo Tarn	1 ½	53			
	Walna Scar Pass	3 ¼	54 ¾			
	Seathwaite	5 ¾	57 ¼			
	Grassguards	8 ¼	59 ¾			
	Penny Hill	11 ½	63			
	Boot	13	64 ½			
	Eskdale Green	3 ¾	68 ¼			
	Hooker Crag	7	71 ½			
	Muncaster Castle	8 ½	73			
	Ravenglass	10 ½	75			

INDEX OF PLACE NAMES ON THE ROUTE MAPS

INDEX OF PLACE NAMES ON THE ROUTE MAPS

INDEX OF PLACE NAMES ON THE ROUTE MAPS

==

Front cover: *The Scafell group across Eskdale*
Coniston Old Man across Coniston Water
Back cover: *The river Kent in Levens Park*
Cartmel
Sunset on the Kent Estuary at Arnside